Wint
Spor

by BRIAN TRUEMAN

Book version by Nicholas Jones

Illustrations from the Cosgrove Hall production
Directed by Jackie Cockle

THAMES METHUEN

First published in Great Britain 1986
by Methuen Children's Books Ltd
11 New Fetter Lane, London EC4P 4EE
in association with Thames Television International Ltd
149 Tottenham Court Road, London W1P 9LL

Designed by Sue Ryall
Printed in Great Britain
ISBN 0 423 01970 8

The unabridged edition of THE WIND IN THE WILLOWS
by Kenneth Grahame is available with full colour illustrations
from the award-winning Cosgrove Hall production.

The Cosgrove Hall film of the original book
by Kenneth Grahame is available on Thames Video

Winter Sports

In the velvet dark of a winter night sky, snow was beginning to fall, the first real snow of the season. It muffled echoes, and hid paths in the Wild Wood. Everywhere, the sharp points of the pines were blunted, square hedgetops rounded, and roof-lines softened.

Mr Toad, warm and snug in his ancestral home, did not notice such a quiet event. He was in bed, reading about his famous ancestors. *Famous Sporting Toads* was a much-read volume. Stimulating as he found it, however, sleep started to creep up on him. He yawned.

'Ah, well! I think I'll call it a day. Brr! Gone quite cold! Wonder if I left the window open . . .'

He went to shut it, and was surprised to find it already closed. But then he noticed flashes of white in the moonlit night.

'Ooh! Snowing! It's snowing! Oh, I say! Where are my . . . ?'

An image from his bed-time reading sprang into his mind, and in an instant he was rooting about in a cupboard. 'Oh, where did I put my . . . ah ha! Skis!'

He dragged them out, relishing the prospect in his imagination:

'Ha! I shall be the famous skiing Toad! Zoom, zoom, zoom, swish! I'll show them all! "Winner of the, er . . . Slocum . . . Mr Toad!" "Hurrah!" "Champion of the Winter Sports . . ." I say! That's it! I'll get 'em *all* doing it! And I shall be the Champion! Ha, ha!' He fell back on the bed, and made his plans.

'That's it! Invitations! First thing in the morning . . . first . . . thing' – he yawned – '. . . in the morning.'

* * *

When morning came, and he awoke to find the skis still on his feet, all the ambitions of the previous day came back. Why wait to get outside? Leaping from his bed, he went out onto the landing to begin the downstairs slalom! 'Yodel-ay-i-tee! Yodel-odel-odel-ay!' But wood against polished wood does not give *quite* the same control as wood on *snow*, and he clattered down the stairs, across the hall, and through the fortunately open door, before he came finally to rest in a snow drift.

Twenty minutes later, more suitably dressed, he set out for Mole's house. Arrived at Mole End, he announced himself cheerily.

'Hello? Mole! Mo-hole! I *say*! Got an invitation! To the Winter Sports!'

There was no reply. 'Oh! Blow! No one here!' he cried, longing to show off to someone. He set off for Ratty's house. What skill, what artistry, he thought! He would be Champion of the Slopes! Lost in such pleasant thoughts, he collided with his second snow-drift of the day.

The journey to Ratty's house promised to be less than smooth, but at last, somewhat damp, somewhat cold and somewhat battered, he arrived.

'Hello! Rat! Ratty! I say! Come on! It's my famous Winter Sports! Oh, bother! Bother and blow! Where *is* everybody?'

The answer was simple: most of the Wildwooders and Riverbankers had been awake for a lot longer than Toad, and had al-

ready discovered the delights of the fresh snow. Rabbits were sliding down the hills on toboggans – or tea-trays if that was all they had. The air was full of

happy sounds, of shrieks and cries of delight. Several hedgehogs were building a snowman. Ratty, Mole and Badger were warming themselves around a brazier.

'I'm surprised Toad hasn't turned up!' remarked Ratty.

'Yes, I can't think *where* he's gone!' agreed Mole. 'I called at Toad Hall on my way here – but there didn't seem to be anyone in!'

'Hmm!' grunted Badger. 'In *bed* more than likely. Slothful creature!'

But just then, as if to repudiate Badger's accusation, a voice called: 'Hello! Hello-o!'

Rat recognised the voice: 'Hello, Toad! Where've you been?' he asked, as the bedraggled animal tottered up.

'Where've *I* been! Where have *I* been! I've been looking for you, that's where I've been. Trudging for miles! If I wasn't rather an expert skier . . . '

Badger cut off Toad's boasting. 'Mole called on you, Toad!'

'And I called on him. *And* Ratty!'

'Well, we were *here*,' Ratty protested.

'Huh! Jolly inconsiderate! I wanted to tell you all about the Winter Sports.'

'Winter Sports?' asked Mole, cautiously.

'Yes! A Grand Competition for all the River Bankers – and the Wildwooders, of course, Badger!' he added hastily.

Unfortunately, the term 'Wildwooders' included not only Badger, but also the Weasels. The Chief Weasel and his Henchman had just come near enough to hear what Toad was saying. 'Good morning, gentlemen!' the Chief announced. Toad jumped, and Badger muttered, 'Oh . . . *you*!'

'My word, Mr Toad! You're looking . . . ' The Chief paused as he searched for the right word to describe Toad's unusual dress. It was somewhat the worse for wear after its tour of the local snow-drifts, but it was undoubtedly . . . er . . . *different*. The Chief eventually decided that 'dapper' was best. His Henchman agreed. 'Yes, very nice, very nice!'

'Ah, yes!' enthused Toad. 'My competition wear, you know!'

Badger groaned, but the Chief was waiting for this cue. 'I *thought* I heard you mention a competition, Mr Toad!'

Mole could see the dangers of any competition in which the *Weasels* took a part. 'I think Mr Toad was talking about some little competitions for the young ones . . . '

Rat was quick on the uptake. '. . . building snow-men . . . ' he added.

'. . . tea-tray races,' continued Mole.

But Toad was not to be diverted. 'No I wasn't!' he snapped.

'Oh, look, Toad . . . !' began Rat . . .

'I wasn't at all! I was talking about a Grand Winter Sports Competition! Skiing!'

Now it was the Weasels' turn to make 'helpful' suggestions: 'Bobsleighs!'

'Down-hill racing!' countered Toad.

'With prizes!' added the Chief.

Toad accepted the idea with alacrity. 'With prizes!' But then he thought a little more. Would *he* have to provide those prizes? 'Eh . . . with *prizes*?'

'Well, naturally the winner would have to have a prize!' declared the Chief.

Toad agreed all too quickly – after all, *he* would win it. 'Oh yes! Yes, I would . . . er . . . *he* would, wouldn't he?'

Rat, forseeing only too well the deep waters Toad was getting into, said firmly, 'Now look, Toad! This is getting silly!'

Badger gave a warning growl: 'Toad!'

'No, no!' enthused Toad. 'I think we *should*

have a race. I shall compete, of course, as Champion of the Slopes.'

'Champion of the Slopes!' exclaimed Mole.

Toad caught a glimpse of Mole's expression, and tried to retrieve the situation. 'No, I mean that whoever *wins* would be Champion of the Slopes.'

'With a prize,' interposed the Chief.

Mole answered quickly, 'Well, we haven't got a prize, so that's that. No cups, no shields, no—'

'A Christmas 'amper!' interrupted the Chief.

'Eh?' Toad hadn't considered that he might have to provide anything.

The Chief continued. 'If anyone can beat my four-man bobsleigh team, I'll give 'em a Christmas 'amper!'

'Oh?' enquired Badger. 'D'you *have* a Christmas hamper?'

'Not yet, Mr Badger, but I'm sure I *will* have,' smirked the Chief, confident that he was going to win. 'If *we* win,' he grinned, '*you* – er – whoever loses, gives *us* a Christmas 'amper!'

'Done!' agreed Toad.

'You will be, Mr Toad, you will — ouch!' The Chief kicked his Henchman.

'Well, I'm having nothing to do with it!' Rat announced, sharply. Mole agreed: 'Nor I!'

Badger added, 'Toad, you're a fool! But you need a lesson in humility . . . '

Toad was indignant. 'There's nothing wrong with *my* humility!'

'. . . so you can have your race! And I'll start you off! Two o'clock sharp, this afternoon!'

'Two o'clock, then, Mr Toad!' smirked the Chief, departing with his henchman.

'Two o'clock!' agreed Toad, also making to move. 'I'll go and wax my alpenstock . . . '

'Foolish creature!' muttered Badger. He took a deep breath, as if to mark the end of one episode and the beginning of the next, and continued, 'Now then, this snowman competition . . . '

* * *

The next hour or two saw a hive of activity, as the snowman competition got underway. Rat and Mole walked about, giving encouragement and making suggestions. 'That's coming along very nicely, Lucy,' the Rat remarked to a young hedgehog, who giggled becomingly, 'Ooh! Thank you, Mr Rat!'

'What are you going to use for eyes?' Mole enquired.

'We've got some chestnuts, Mr Mole! Haven't we, Billy?'

'Well, er . . . um . . . ' replied a sheepish-looking Billy, mouth full of chestnuts.

'Ooh! Billy! Just go and get some more!'

Rat and Mole laughed as they watched Billy trudging back to the edge of the clearing. Just then, another young Rabbit arrived, evidently upset. 'Sir! Please, Sir!'

'Hello, young fellow! What's the trouble?'

'Please, Sir! They've stolen our carrot!'

'Stolen your carrot!' exclaimed Mole.

'It was for the snowman's nose, Sir, and they've stolen it!'

'*Who've* stolen it?'

'*Them*, Sir!' Mole turned to follow the Rabbit's gaze, and saw two Weasels, building an evil-looking snowman.

Rat said brightly, 'Come on, Mole!' The two went towards the Weasels. Rat continued con-

fidently as they approached:

'Now then, you lot!'

With an expression of utter innocence, the nearest Weasel looked up. 'Eh?'

'What do you think you're doing?'

'We're building a snowman, that's what we're doing – and we're minding our own business an' all.'

'Don't you be impertinent!' reproved Mole.

'Oh, yes?' sneered an older Weasel.

'And give this lad his carrot back!' instructed Rat.

'We 'aven't got his—'

'At once!'

'Oh, all right!' The older Weasel threw the carrot insolently at Rat, hissing at the Rabbit, 'You wait, son!'

Mole, trying to make light of that threat, remarked brightly, 'Don't you worry young 'un! Here you are; here's your Snowman's nose!'

'Thank you, Mr Mole!' The Rabbit scampered back to his snowman.

Rat turned back to the Weasels. 'Aren't you and your friends a bit old for a snowman competition?'

'Oh yes? Where's it say *that* in the rules?'

'Don't be silly! There are no rules!' replied Mole.

'Well, then!' sneered the Weasel. 'We haven't broken them then, 'ave we?'

Rat found it difficult to answer that effectively, and had to say lamely, 'Just no more bullying, that's all – or I'll see you off myself! Come on Mole! They've got another ten minutes before we judge them.' He paused. 'Mmm! Nearly time for the Great Downhill Race.'

'Huh!' said Mole, remembering Toad's boastfulness, and fearing what might befall that conceited animal.

* * *

Well might the Mole be fearful, for Toad was having a few minor difficulties with his skis, not helped by the Weasels, who were preparing their bobsleigh nearby. Toad was adjusting his goggles, and trying to restrain his ski-poles, which seemed to have a life of their own. They caught between his legs, poked him in the eye, and generally refused to be where he wanted them. Thus occupied, he did not notice a Weasel creep up behind him, and attach a string to one ski. The other end was tied to a tree. Toad might set off down the hill, but he would not be taking all his equipment to the bottom . . .

Badger strode towards the competitors, 'Now then, two o'clock precisely!' He looked towards the Chief Weasel. 'You got your team together yet?' he enquired.

As he spoke, a Weasel gave a clandestine thumbs-up to his Chief, who replied confidently to Badger. 'Right, Mr Badger! We're ready!'

'Toad! You ready?'

'Oh, yes, Badger! Ha ha! looking forward to a Christmas Hamper! Ha ha ha ha! Yodel-ay-ee-tee!'

'Hmmm!' said Badger, under his breath, and then aloud, 'Stand by then! I shall say "Ready, set, go!". That clear?'

'Yes!' shouted all the Weasels and Toad, confidently together.

'Right! Ready . . . set . . . go!'

Four Weasels, Toad, a bobsleigh, two skis and two poles set off down the hill. But they were not to remain together for long. Toad was in fine downhill style, poles tucked up under his arms, when the string tautened and his left ski disappeared behind him. 'Waagh!' He may have lost control, but he certainly didn't lose speed. He continued his downhill rush, and the Weasels, safe – or so they thought – in their bobsleigh, laughed at the success of their plot. Then *their* conveyance hit a bump, and took off into the air. 'Whoaaaa!' they shouted in a chorus of panic. The bob careered onwards and downwards, but its four occupants found themselves left hanging in the branches of a tree. Toad too, came to rest . . . in a particularly large snowdrift.

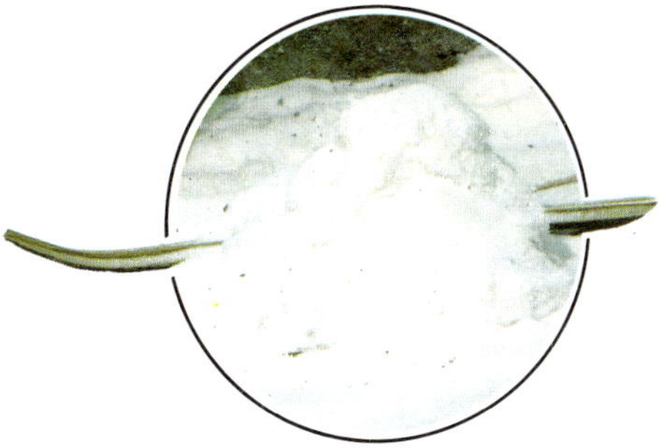

Back at the snowmen, judging was in progress. Rat and Mole were examining the Rabbits' efforts. 'Very good, Sonny!'

'Yes! Ha! that carrot makes all the difference! Very good!' said Mole.

'Cor! Thanks!' said Billy, overwhelmed by such praise.

Rat and Mole moved onto the next snowman. It was the Weasels', and as they approached, Rat remarked, 'I'm sorry to say, Mole, it's the best yet.'

'But those Weasels are much older than the youngsters!'

'Yes, but they were right. There are no rules, so I can't disqualify them. So, unless we find a *better* one . . .'

'Oh dear!' agreed Mole, turning towards the final snowman. It was Lucy's . . . and it was magnificent. 'Oh, my goodness!'

'What?' Rat turned, and saw. 'By jove, Lucy! That's brilliant!' She was standing by a sculpture of Toad, incredibly life-like . . . and standing on one ski . . .

Mole agreed. 'My goodness, yes! No doubt who that's meant to be!'

Lucy had not, of course, built that particular snowman, and being a well-brought-up and therefore thoroughly honest little Hedgehog, did not want to take the credit

for something not of her making, 'Please Sir! It isn't meant to be anyone!'

But Rat, mistaking honesty for modesty, laughed indulgently.

'Well, that's it, isn't it, Rat? That's the one!' said Mole.

'Oh yes! That's the winner.'

Lucy, confused but grateful, could only say, 'Oooh!'

Mole and the surrounding crowd applauded. 'Come along Lucy,' he said, 'there's some treacle toffee for you – and for the others!'

Amidst general cheers of delight, Mole turned to Rat. 'I suppose we'll have to give the Weasels some too?'

'Well,' Rat said, 'like Toad, they seem to have disappeared!'

'Yes,' mused Mole. 'I wonder what's become of Toad!'

They set off towards the brazier, too soon to see the Snowman-Toad begin to move. It blinked, and lumps of snow dropped from its face. It shook a limb or two, and hunks of snow fell off . . .

* * *

When Rat and Mole reached the fire, they found Badger and all the young animals grouped around it. Mole remarked to Badger, 'What a splendid day it's been . . . '

'Like old times,' agreed Badger. 'Ha! Like old times!'

'Yes, I must say . . . ' began Rat. 'Hello! Who's that?! In the distance, he could see a figure pulling a sledge. On it was a hamper.

'Hello, you chaps!' said Toad, as he came within range.

'Hello, Toad!' Rat greeted him brightly. Badger

said, suspiciously, 'Toad! Where've you been?'

To Mole, there was only one important matter. 'Who won the race, Toad?'

'Race? Oh, blow the silly old race! Who cares about racin'! No, no! I lost interest, that's all!'

'Do you mean you lost the race?' asked Rat, suspiciously.

'Oh, I say!' replied the indignant animal. 'No, I just got involved in . . . other things!'

'But . . . ' began Rat. Toad, however, wasn't going to let himself be cross-examined too closely. He added quickly, 'But I thought we *all* deserved a prize – so I popped home and got – a Christmas Hamper!'

Under the general clamour of approval and thanks, Badger muttered to Mole, 'Good heavens! You don't suppose he's learned a lesson, do you?'

'He might have, Badger, he might have!'

And they turned and watched the subject of their considerations encouraging all his guests to enjoy his generosity: 'Come on, all of you! Dip in! Dip in!'

* * *

The short winter's day neared its end. The flames in the brazier seemed to brighten as the pale sun lessened and the fading shadows lengthened. The velvet blue-black of a calm winter night crept up on the happy group of Fieldmice, Rabbits and Hedgehogs. Rat, Mole and Badger watched over them amiably. Only the Weasels stayed away, not daring to face the consequences of their underhand attempt to win the Great Downhill Race. And the would-be Champion of the Slopes almost forgot his ambitions in the joy of the happy gathering.

UNITED WE STAND

United We Stand

BOB MONCUR
with John Gibson

PELHAM BOOKS

First published in Great Britain by
PELHAM BOOKS LTD
52 *Bedford Square*
*London, W.C.*1
1971

7207 0435 9

Set and printed in Great Britain by
Tonbridge Printers Ltd
Peach Hall Works, Tonbridge, Kent
in Times ten on twelve point on paper
supplied by P. F. Bingham Ltd, and bound
by James Burn at Esher, Surrey

Contents

Illustrations

Acknowledgements

The author and publishers gratefully acknowledge permission to reproduce the following photographs: *Daily Express*, 12, 15, 17; *Daily Mail*, 4, 14; *Newcastle Journal*, 3, 6, 7, 9, 16, 18; *Syndication International*, 19; *Western Mail*, 1

Foreword

by

Joe Harvey

Bob Moncur has got the job I enjoyed for years: captaining the greatest club on earth, Newcastle United. And I couldn't think of a better player to do it.

In soccer today more than ever before dedication and courage must be mingled with class if a player is to reach the very top. Bob has balanced the three perfectly and added the extra ingredient of natural leadership which has rightly made him the new skipper of Scotland.

In a nutshell, Moncur is my kind of player, and I don't mind admitting it. I know when he goes on the field that I can rely on him accepting responsibility and exercising the necessary authority.

He is a team man through and through. The title of his book, *United We Stand*, emphasises that better than I can.

Moncur's story is one which had to be told and he does it with honesty and not a little humour.

He doesn't let me forget, either, that I once nearly sold him when his growth temporarily seemed to halt. I count it as one of my breaks that he didn't go.

Since then he has developed into the supreme sweeper and a most valuable asset both to Newcastle United and Scotland.

I wish him equal success in his new venture.

1 My Greatest Hour

The time was exactly 8.43 p.m. on Thursday, May 29, 1969, the second when the whole world stood still for Bob Moncur, the lad from Perth who had once almost become a soccer has-been.

I can still remember the scene now simply because I don't want to ever forget it. Gallowgate was packed to capacity, almost like a Christmas stocking about to burst at the seams. Nearly 60,000 people were crammed inside and high above the popular side kids, arms outstretched for balance, picked their way along the roof tops risking their very lives to get a better view. The boss, Joe Harvey, told us later that he had never seen anything like it since the early fifties when Newcastle United were lifting the F.A. Cup as regularly as clockwork.

It was the first leg of the European Fairs' Cup final and Ujpest Dozsa, the crack Magyars, were facing us across the battlefield. We had all been told that the Hungarians were invincible – hadn't they beaten England's best side, Leeds United, home and away in a previous round? And hadn't soccer's aristocrats like Don Revie, Bill Shankly and Jock Stein lined up firmly behind Ujpest in their predictions?

Certainly the white-clad men from Budapest were making a fair job of keeping a clean sheet. For sixty-three minutes they had kept it tight at the back, slowed it down, and played it around in midfield. Possession football we call it and in skipper Janoc Gorocs they had a wily old fox who excelled at the game.

The boss, sitting alongside coach Dave Smith in the dug-out, was getting impatient as he bit on his umpteenth fag. He knew we must take a lead, and a good 'un, to Budapest with us for the return. And time was running out.

In an effort to get more penetration up front substitute Alan Foggon was waved on to the track to begin warming up as we won a free-kick just outside the box.

Normally I stay at the back: I'm the destroyer, paid for my strength, my ability to sweep up behind the defence and my knack of being able to read a game. I spend a lot of my time between Iam McFaul and our 18-yard line.

But this was different. We just HAD to get a break. So up I went in an effort to lend height and weight to our attack.

Gibbo lofted the free-kick to the back of the box as he so often does for big Wyn Davies. Wyn, one of the few centre-forwards who still likes to use his chest to bring a ball down, breasted it forward and as the tall, black-clad Szentimihalyi came out hammered the ball against him. I could see the rebound zooming towards me like a satellite in outer space and I knew I must burst the net. I drew back my left foot and connected as sweet as you like.

At that precise moment the whole world stood still for me. I had never scored a competitive goal for United's senior side in my life and suddenly here I was in a European final engulfed by the throaty, almost hysterical roar of 60,000 Geordies.

They tell me I didn't show much emotion apart from raising my arm high into the sky. Maybe not. I'm not the sort who can run the length of the field in excitement.

But I feel it – deep down inside. My heart pounds and my pulses race just like anyone else's.

As I ran back for the kick-off my thoughts turned fleetingly to the stand where I knew my father and wife Camille were sitting. I bet they are feeling great, I thought.

The old man's a lot like me. Afterwards he's nonchalant, dismissing things in a casual manner. But inside he gets burned up. And I have him to thank for stopping me chucking in my hand as a kid and returning to Scotland.

But the match, or should I say the tie, was far from won. One goal wouldn't be enough to defeat Ujpest and we all knew it. With Foggon on for little Jackie Sinclair we poured forward with renewed vigour.

The ground beneath our feet almost trembled with the roar of voices which must have carried for miles on the night air. I don't know what it must have done to the Hungarians but I know what it did to us. It turned us all into giants.

I thought I'd had my personal moment of triumph but unbelievably I scored again only ten minutes later. Moving forward from left-half with Ujpest backing off, I played a one-two with Ben Arentoft to get within about 20 or 25 yards of the goal.

Suddenly the ball stood up in front of me after hitting a divot. I was about to shoot when Jim Scott ran across me. I hesitated thinking he was going to hit it but he shouted to me to have a go and I just let fly. The ball hardly lifted as it flashed right across the box and into the far corner of the net.

I reckon the boss nearly ricked his neck trying to see the No. 6 on my back to confirm what his eyes had just seen. My scoring two goals at all, never mind in a European final, was just too much for him. Who said the days of miracles are over?

I saw the television recording of the goal afterwards. As I returned to the middle the cameras zoomed in on me – and there I was with my arms spread wide and a look on my face that seemed to say to all the world: 'It's easy really.' I had to laugh.

Frank Clark, who normally scores as regularly as me which is never, came over with a grin splitting his face.

'You lucky devil,' he said, 'that shot must have bounced eight times before it went in!'

Actually it did bounce twice but it counted and that was enough for me. The sound of two goals had a marvellous ring about it.

We still kept going after that because in these two-legged ties it doesn't matter how many a team may score they must get more. Setubal had learned me that lesson if I didn't already know it. We hammered them 5–1 at Gallowgate yet almost got knocked out in Portugal.

With the crowd on the verge of delirium we managed a third goal before the final whistle went. Jim Scott's goal was one of the most courageous I've ever known one of our forwards score and it came from a man noted more for his frills than his brawn.

Another one-two with Arentoft left the keeper favourite for the ball in a race with Scotty. But the Hungarian made a fatal mistake hesitating for a split second and Jim, carried on the tidal wave of emotion rolling down from the terraces, galloped on blindly to get his toe to the ball before tumbling over the prostrate body of the keeper.

He could have been badly injured as a result of his courage but thankfully he was not.

In the excitement of our second-half push for goals big Wyn Davies fractured his cheekbone – on the back of my head!

He must have been a bit upset about it as later he wrote in a newspaper article that it happened because I was over anxious to complete my hat-trick.

At the risk of disappointing you, Wyn, I must say that isn't strictly true. I wasn't trying to pinch your thunder in your own territory. In fact I never saw you or knew you were there until I felt the thump.

What happened was that I went into the Ujpest penalty box for a dead-ball kick because I thought our attack needed a little extra strength. The ball was dropped short to the nearest post and rather than see it go loose I made an effort to reach it and actually got my head to it. Suddenly there was a crash and I could feel a cheek crunching into the back of my head. When I turned round it was Wyn.

The Budapest return, funnily enough, was to bring me that hat-trick Davies was on about and complete a triumph I would never have dared dream of. Forwards don't even contemplate three goals in a European cup final, never mind defenders.

Looking back, my goal behind the Iron Curtain must rate as my most cherished for two reasons. First, I believe it was the most important as we were two goals down at the time and looked in grave danger of sacrificing the trophy. And secondly to me it was also the best executed of the three.

The first-half, or at least the first half hour, went well enough. Ujpest attacked with flair and imagination just as we expected them to but we survived with a few frights which our style of play will always bring.

Then just as I felt that the fire in their bellies was beginning to die they got a goal that was tinged with a little bit of luck. A pass struck the outstretched boot of Frank Clark and was diverted into the path of Bene. A ramrod shot from one of Europe's most respected forwards did the rest.

To make matters worse we gave away a bad goal before half-time to go in two down. Gorocs was allowed to gallop through our defence on the right flank without any challenge and he beat McFaul from close in.

I had to fight back the tears as I trudged off the field. I was utterly convinced that we had lost . . . I would never get my hands on that trophy now. All the other lads felt the same. The dressing-room was like a morgue.

Joe Harvey was already there as we entered. But instead of a blistering attack which we all expected he spoke quietly and calmly. I think he sensed how sick we were and realised that angry aggression would only dampen us further. Instead he pointed out that we were still leading 3–2 after one hundred and thirty-five minutes soccer. All we needed was one goal and Ujpest would die, he stressed.

Incredibly we got it within a minute of the restart and I was lucky enough to be the scorer again. A corner on the left saw Szentimihalyi punch out under pressure. Sinclair picked up the loose ball to return it inside the area where I was lurking after going up for the flag kick. The ball was actually curling away from me as I swung round but I still connected with my left. From the moment my foot touched the ball I knew I had scored. It felt so good – like hitting a perfect iron on the golf course. The full-back standing on the line desperately tried to get a hand to the speeding ball but he had no real chance.

I'd got three goals with my left foot which wasn't bad for a right-footed player!

After that things happened so fast that my biggest job was keeping up with the score. Away goals counting double in the event of a tie on aggregate really confuses things in the heat of the battle and I spent most of my time trying to work out the latest position with Frank Clark.

It was like one of those old comedy films. I would rush up to Frank and shout: 'How many have they to get now, Frank?' and minutes later when he passed he would yell back: 'Four I think.'

Just after Dave Smith signalled from the touchline that there were only five minutes left with us leading 3–2 Clark, with a mischievous glint in his eye, said: 'I reckon we can do it now Bob if we keep our heads!' A 6–2 aggregate lead certainly proved enough.

To be truthful, Ujpest disappointed me. Once we had scored they folded up and died completely. I would hate to think that we would ever do that.

What made it more baffling was that the way they were playing they still had a fair chance but it became so easy for us that we were able to kick the ball about as in a five-a-side game. We have never been a pure footballing side like Spurs but especially in the last ten minutes we literally toyed with the opposition and the crowd rose to us. It was our final triumph. Everyone wanted to do his little tricks. No pass had to be more than ten yards as we kept the ball and went into our routine.

When the final whistle went I made a point of shaking hands with the unhappy Ujpest players before letting my emotions flood in. It's just a small personal point but I've always felt that it is terribly disrespectful when the winners jump on each other and completely ignore the players they have just beaten.

I received the trophy from FIFA president Sir Stanley Rous but for the life of me I cannot remember a word he said. Everything was just a haze. I do recall a couple of the boys grabbing me and roughly lifting me on their shoulders but all I could think of was our fans. In the second-half as we fought back we could always hear their voices piercing the wall of Ujpest noise and it was to them that we owed a special salute.

So before we began our lap of honour we ran over to where our supporters were yelling themselves hoarse in the stand and gave them a long look at the trophy.

During the run round the track I was striding out in front oblivious to almost everything but the silver pot glinting in my hand in front of me when suddenly I heard a pained voice from the back. 'Take your time,' groaned Clarky. 'I can't flippin' keep up with you!'

The world and his brother seemed to be running round with us and in another few strides I saw Eileen McFaul jump on Iam. Before I could blink I felt someone on my back and immediately panicked. I've always hated being smothered and I thought some of the supporters were about to mob us.

'Hey, get off!' I shouted, shrugging my shoulder in an effort to untangle myself from my attacker. Only then could I see it was Camille. The wives had somehow clambered down from the stand and got onto the pitch. I'm afraid that to my eternal embarrassment the first thing I said was: 'How the hell did you get here?'

The celebrations really got under way back in the dressing-room. The boss was fifty that day and we gave him a rousing chorus of 'happy birthday' while he stood with his clenched fist high in the air, victory style.

I grabbed the long banana-shaped trophy and gulped down a mouthful of champagne which had been poured into it. Champagne spilled and splashed over the front of my shirt to mingle with the sweat of ninety minutes' work. Next it was Stan Seymour who took the cup. The man who had shared in so many F.A. Cup triumphs with United just stood there and let the champagne saturate his good suit. 'Aye,' he said, drying his mouth. 'That's grand!'

It was like drinking a yard of ale – almost impossible – but no one was going to complain especially the dry cleaners who were going to do a roaring trade.

That night we were to burn the midnight oil back in our

hotel on Margaret Island in the middle of the River Danube but first there was an official reception for both teams.

I think the boss and Lord Westwood worked it but whatever the reason the speeches were kept to a minimum so that we could leave as quickly as was respectfully possible. We were all dying to join our wives and the Press lads for a party.

The collecting of our winners' medals (or should I say miniature trophies) had none of the pomp of Wembley. I simply put all the awards from Sir Stanley Rous on a big tray and said: 'Anyone want one?' They quickly went.

David Macbeth, the TV singer who is a great fan of ours, got the party off to a swinging start. He climbed up on a table and gave us song upon song. After that we all had a go and if the standard deteriorated rapidly we were all too happy to notice.

Although nearly all the champagne the doc had craftily brought on the plane in readiness had been drunk in the dressing-room, the club spared no expense at the party. I just kept on ordering on behalf of the boys.

Eventually sometime around four or five o'clock in the morning the pop-eyed barmaid had only three bottles left apart from some French champagne which she said cost many dollars.

'How many *pounds*?' I asked. 'Nine pounds a bottle,' she replied. 'That's all right. I'll take them,' I said in my best voice. There was so many of us at the party and we were all so happy that we drank the champagne without anyone feeling in the least ill. After a long season in which we had won a European trophy at the first attempt the elation carried us along.

I had given the trophy to Joe Richardson before the party started for safe keeping which from hindsight was a wise thing to do. For later in the year when it was entrusted to the boss and me, we lost it.

It happened at the BBC TV Sports Personality of the Year award in London when we appeared with the cup. The programme was screened on a Thursday night and as we were playing on the Saturday we never had a drink at the studios, so no one can blame that for our dilemma.

The next day I strolled into the club offices after morning training.

'Did you have a good night last night?' our assistant secretary Malcolm Hoole asked casually.

'Aye, canny,' I said.

'Got the cup?'

A feeling of numbness started in the pit of my stomach and crept rapidly over my body. Not only had we forgotten the Fairs' Cup but I couldn't remember where we had left it. Luckily a phone call to the television studios confirmed that they had it and it was hurriedly put on a train north.

I've never felt so relieved in my life.

2 What Europe Means

The Fairs' Cup. To a lot of people it might be the poor man's competition trailing as it does behind the big European Champions' Cup. But to Newcastle United and to Tyneside it spells magic ... a magic that fills grounds with people and hearts with anticipation.

For three years now we've been carrying on a love affair with the Fairs' Cup and it's got to the stage where we daren't think of a season without its stimulus.

Tyneside has always been an area saturated with soccer interest. Put a row of black and white shirts out to dry at Gallowgate and you'll get 10,000 people along to watch them. But since Europe opened its doors in 1968 we have got to know a new, big, bright, world full of exciting places and interesting people. Our horizons have become so much wider and the public have flocked to St James's in ever larger numbers. Teams like Feyenoord, Ujpest Dozsa, Inter Milan, Real Zaragoza and Sporting Lisbon – world famous but never before seen at Gallowgate – have suddenly become almost as familiar as Arsenal or Spurs. Top internationals previously seen flitting across the TV screen on odd occasions are now flesh and blood like the rest of us. Inter's World Cup stars Mazzola, Facchetti, Burgnich and Boninsegna, Ujpest's legendary striker Ferenc Bene, the Flying Dutchman of Anderlecht Jan Mulder, Feyenoord's slim Swede Ove Kindvall ... all have come within the compass of United's fans.

Yet outside the North-east our entry season after season has been a bit of a joke. We've qualified by finishing tenth, ninth and seventh in the First Division table thanks to an assortment of reasons which have caused some sly sniggers round the country.

The controversial one-club-one-city rule has been our biggest ally, of course, but there have been other factors. The first year Manchester United helped us by winning the European Cup and so qualifying again. Then we made it a hat-trick of appearances when Derby County were banned from Europe because of alleged irregularities in their books.

Backdoor entrants: that's what they said about us. And it hurt even if it was true. We hadn't bent the rules or crawled in on our bellies. We'd merely played forty-two matches and found at the end of it that someone was ready to hand us a prize. What were we supposed to do – refuse it?

The jibes, in fact, spurred us on. Those who chose to ridicule found that we had the last laugh as we rammed their words down their throats.

For a team not good enough for Europe we have done pretty well. We won the Cup at the first attempt while the big fish like Leeds, Liverpool and Chelsea floundered. And then we reached the quarter-finals next time round which meant a run of twenty consecutive games in Europe before bending the knee.

In our third season we got Inter Milan, twice world club champions, at the first hurdle and dumped them as well. Perhaps we are a cup team or just a bunch of unpredictables but whatever the reason we have pleased the folk who matter – the 60,000 or so Geordies who put their cash down to see us topple the cream of the Continent.

And what moments there have been. The torrential rain of Lisbon when the substitutes' bench began to float; the snow-storm when we caught Setubal cold and the carnival night when they made us dance in the return; New Year in Zaragoza; the Rangers riot that brought questions in the House of Commons; the horror of Anderlecht's last-minute winner as our fans sang songs of victory; and the unbelievable exhibition of Inter Milan.

In the main the memories are easily split into two: those

caused by the weather and those caused by incidents either on the field or in the crowd.

My European debut falls into the first category. I'd missed United's opening two matches with Feyenoord because of a cartilage operation although I jetted to Rotterdam with our fans and sat in agony in the stand as the lads faced wave upon wave of Feyenoord attacks.

A splendid 4–0 first leg win eventually got us through and on the day the rains came to Lisbon I was back as skipper against Sporting, a club steeped in tradition. The match was in the magnificent Jose Alvalade Stadium, a huge concrete bowl housing a dozen sports and its own mini hotel. It towered almost gloatingly over a shanty town where raggy, dirty little urchins lived in the same wooden huts with chickens and goats. This blatant contradiction of life startled me at first but as we continued to move around the Continent I soon got used to the sight of the rich living apparently unconcerned on the doorstep of the poor.

I was a little apprehensive of facing Sporting with a team including a couple of unseasoned kids – Winstanley and Foggon – and me in a No. 10 shirt ready to drop back and bolster the defence. The plan was for me to go straight into the back four and Burton, wearing my normal No. 6, to take the middle of the park unless the game dictated a more defensive outlook.

In fact it didn't. Young Winstanley, who I always thought was under-rated at Gallowgate, was as steady as a rock and we led through a Scott goal until ten seconds from time. Then Morais, a chunky player who stopped Pele in the 1966 World Cup, managed to lift his right foot out of the gluey morass and swing it at the ball with no more than hope in his heart. From thirty yards the ball lifted and then dropped to be pushed on to the bar by McFaul only for it to rebound, strike Willie on the back of the arm, and drop over the line. Sporting had denied us victory but only until the second leg when a Robson special wrapped things up.

The Lisbon match had been played to the accompaniment of rolling thunder and bright flashes of lightning which brought a dramatic effect but left us absolutely saturated. It was like playing under a shower turned full on and in a paddyfield. The downpour also revealed the flaw in the Continent's super stadiums. They are all uncovered and on nights like this the spectator is left to the mercy of the heavens.

Poor Wyn Davies. When the storm began and everyone scampered from the substitutes' bench the boss pinched big Wyn's overcoat and put it on. But the rain was so heavy that it wet the coat right through to the lining. The big fella was absolutely sick!

After easing out Real Zaragoza (the best team we met in our Cup-winning year, incidentally) we ran into some more freak weather against our second Portuguese opponents Vitoria Setubal. They came to Gallowgate to meet us on a pitch covered in snow and with a blizzard raging. Talk about the odds being loaded against you: some of their lads hadn't seen the white fluffy stuff in their lives before. They were absolutely bemused.

Despite the blizzard which had gripped the city for a couple of days the Geordies showed exactly what the Fairs' Cup means to them. Nearly 58,000 turned up to watch us demoralise the poor Portuguese 5–1.

It wasn't a contest and their little coloured winger Jacinto Joao, after playing in gloves, finally trudged off during the second-half completely beaten by the weather.

What a different tale it was in the return. We were once again back at the Jose Alvalade because Setubal, a small fishing town a few miles south of Lisbon, could not house a big game with its stadium being rebuilt. A four-goal lead should have been big enough to make things comfortable but unknown to us we were about to encounter for the first time the sort of distractions which are part and parcel of the European scene.

Setubal, the crafty devils, arranged a carnival. Clowns and men wearing huge, grotesque masks paraded and jigged round the pitch. Others played saxophones and beat big drums. Flags were waved constantly from a motor bike and sidecar that roared round and round the athletic track. And all the time we fought to retain our first-leg lead.

Setubal, under their conditions, were a dangerous side and none more so than Jacinto Joao, the little winger who had hated it at the park. Just to make things more difficult, when they snatched two goals in two minutes in the second-half to lead 3–1 and scented victory, they really began to mix it. We were spit upon, hacked and punched. Young Foggon was clubbed to the ground and then kicked as he lay in agony and I watched in horror as Ollie Burton, taken off a few minutes earlier, leaped from the subs' bench and raced towards the incident. Luckily it was so far away he was able to cool down, otherwise I'm sure he would have got himself into big trouble.

Some time later the Liverpool players told me that when they played there the following season Setubal did exactly the same thing – put on a carnival, the lot. And this time it worked. Liverpool lost on the two legs through the away goals rule.

The two really violent matches we've had in Europe were still to come, of course. One was in the next round, the semi-final, against Glasgow Rangers and the other against the great Inter Milan, a couple of seasons later. Both were at Gallowgate but there was a significant difference. The Rangers riot was strictly a thing with the fans. The match was hard but completely fair.

Inter unbelievably lost their heads and in the end some players appeared to concentrate merely on kicking lumps out of us. Wyn Davies and Tommy Gibb in particular were used like punchbags. It was all very sad to see a club of their tradition and esteem react in this way. When we drew them we felt it an honour, but the way they disintegrated in the face of defeat left a bad taste in the mouth.

But let's not jump the gun. First there was Rangers and our passport to our first final. A 0–0 draw at Ibrox in front of a record Fairs' Cup attendance of 75,580 was highlighted by a tremendous penalty save by McFaul from Andy Penman.

Naturally Gallowgate was packed for the return and the atmosphere was tense, almost explosive. It took us the first-half to master it with little football of note and then we opened up to crack two goals through Scott and Sinclair.

Rangers were as good as out. And that was the signal. The police and club had had enough sense to segregate the fans but it wasn't to be enough. Rangers' mob, penned in at the Gallowgate end like baying wolves, let go a hail of bottles that flew over our heads as we defended the Gallowgate goal. My blood ran cold. I could hear the pounding of feet behind me as the first of the yobs came over the top and poured on to the pitch.

A swift gesture from referee John Gow, a Swansea schoolmaster, and we were all sprinting like mad for the safety of the tunnel. There the Rangers players stood with their heads bowed in shame as their fans fought and brawled with police dogs and their handlers in the centre of the pitch while, thankfully, our fans stayed on the terraces. God knows what would have happened if one of our lot had set foot on the battle area.

It took seventeen minutes for police to push the hooligans back and stack the hundreds of bottles by the touchline so that the game could be finished. And each minute must have been humiliating to both the Rangers players and officials. They acted sensibly and correctly throughout. It is hardly their fault that they have inherited so many idiots.

The match with Inter was the most violent in which I've played. Surprisingly the first leg in the vast San Siro Stadium had gone quietly enough. We played really well and led through a courageous header from Davies until six minutes from time when Cella, their balding, little sweeper, moved up to score from the edge of the box.

The return was just as placid . . . until I scored! With half an hour gone we won a corner on the left and I went forward to take the near post. Robson swung the ball across and as I moved out so did their keeper Vieri. I got there first and plonked a header well wide of him. Although Cella almost tied himself in knots trying to one-hand the ball away it was a goal right enough.

Inside a minute the balloon went up. Vieri collected a ball by the post and Davies moved forward to challenge. Wyn didn't, in fact, touch the keeper but the Italian obviously thought he was going to and elbowed him roughly in the chest. The referee promptly awarded a free-kick. In true Latin fashion all hell was let loose. The referee, Joseph Minnoy of Belgium, was surrounded by angry, gesticulating Inter players and then dropped by a short, sharp underarm punch. I couldn't believe my eyes!

When things were eventually sorted out the keeper was sent off and all chance of a football match had gone out of the window. Inter were fuming and ready for a fight. What big Wyn had to do with the keeper's departure I don't know but the Italians obviously blamed him for their predicament and picked him out for special treatment.

Even some of their top stars who a few months before had graced our television screens in that epic World Cup final against Brazil in Mexico went wild.

Wyn was kneed in the small of the back, then punched in the face, drawing blood. Gibbo was knocked out with as crisp a punch as you'll see at the Albert Hall. How on earth more Italians weren't sent off I'll never know. It got so bad that at the height of the brawling I twice ran fifteen yards or more to the touchline for conferences with the boss.

Most of the crowd must have wondered what was going on. Well, I'll tell you. The first time I asked the gaffer whether, with us leading 2–0 and virtually through, he had considered taking Davies off for his own good. I felt that Wyn couldn't go on walking away from provocation and might be goaded into retaliation with the threat of him being sent off. That way we would have lost him for the first leg of the next round. The boss decided against it mainly because Davies had 'em rattled – he headed our second goal – and he was doing his job magnificently but it was touch and go.

Our second touchline pow-wow only a few minutes later might sound a little shocking now but at the time I can assure you it was the sane and sensible thing to do. I asked for police protection – not from the fans but from the Italian players! Feelings were running so high that there was a distinct possibility of trouble at the final whistle and I asked the boss to get police stationed down the tunnel to eliminate the chance of a punch-up. Remember that only a couple of weeks before Lazio of Rome had beaten up the Arsenal players after another niggly Fairs' Cup tie. Italy *v.* England wasn't going to become a regular feature as fight of the week.

Why Inter had to resort to such tactics at all beats me. They have talented players who are capable of taking on the best. Strong-arm tactics are totally unnecessary.

Scare stories are always part of the European scene, of course. And how the Press boys love 'em. A couple of injuries, or an illness on an away trip and it can keep them going in good, readable copy right up to kick-off time. But it's not so funny for the players concerned. I've experienced it twice and that's enough for me.

Against F.C. Porto in Portugal I spent all my time staring at the four walls of my hotel room from a position flat on my back in bed and when we played Anderlecht in Brussels I hurt my knee in a kickabout and played virtually on one leg. The Porto business was a real wierd experience. I didn't feel too frisky when we jetted out and hardly touched my food. If I remember rightly I only had a bowl of soup. The next day we were all due to visit a nearby holiday resort for a meal and by the time I got to the hotel I was in a heck of a state. While the boys ate I curled up and went to sleep on a chair. The doc had to wake me up – and did that start a panic! I had obviously picked up some mystery stomach bug and was whipped back to headquarters and straight up to my room. Dosed with pills I went back to sleep only to wake up a few hours later with the sheets ringing wet with sweat. It was so bad the bed had to be changed.

Not only was I supposed to be playing in a European cup-tie twenty-four hours later but I was also supposed to be substitute goalkeeper. John Hope was injured and so for once we had travelled without any cover for McFaul. As I usually went between the posts in training I was elected Willie's deputy. I learned later that the boss gave up the ghost when my bed needed changing. He told the Press I had no chance. But as quickly as the bug struck me it left. That same night, although very weak, I ate a reasonable meal in my room and the next morning – the day of the match – I trained with the boys.

While the papers had a field day over my dilemma Camille was acting out a drama of her own back at home. Worried over the stories of my illness, she smashed up my car in a spectacular crash which saw her airborne for 15 yards. Her mind must have been in a turmoil as she flew out to see the match.

I felt a little better a few hours before the kick-off and walked round to the supporters' hotel with Ollie to see our wives. Camille was sitting there with Sue Burton looking as happy as Larry and tremendously relieved at my apparent recovery. I hadn't an inkling that anything was wrong although Sue told Ollie about the car crash while my back was turned. The girls didn't want to give me an extra burden before a big game and for that I am eternally grateful.

We got a good result (a 0–0 draw) and I was in a great mood as I nipped across the city with Ollie and the boss to see the girls again. After a few minutes Camille said: 'Bob, I want to see you outside.' Puzzled I followed her. 'I've had a bump in your car,' she said and then before I could reply added: 'The police think it could be a write-off.'

It was a brand new car with only 5,000 miles on the clock but I was so relieved that we were both all right and so elated at the result that all I could say was: 'Ah well, it was needing a wash anyway!' Camille reckons that if we hadn't got a good result she would never have told me.

In Brussels two rounds later it was an injury and not illness that overtook me. The day before the game I was playing in goal during a practice match and hurt my knee. It went up like a balloon and the doc suggested I had an injection for the game but I was too much of a coward and went out with no protection.

The trouble was that both our full-backs, Craig and Clark,

had been left behind in England because of injuries and with me on one leg we were in a bit of a mess at the back. Had the back four been at full strength I would have got through okay with a little help but as it was the others were too busy trying to do their own jobs to give me any cover. Anderlecht boasted a great attack, too, and to be truthful we were a little lucky to get away with a 2–0 defeat.

The second leg is now history, of course. We played brilliantly in front of a full house to lead 3–0 with our fans singing throatily of victory when Anderlecht broke away a minute from time to score out of the blue. That one kick wrenched the Fairs' Cup cruelly from our grasp at the height of our triumph. We were out on the away goals rule.

The agony and the ecstasy of Europe was never better portrayed than in those last fateful moments. Europe, because of the immense drama it throws up, has become our lifeblood. It is like a breath of fresh air to both the players and the fans. We aim to keep it that way for as long as possible.

3 My First Cap

Playing for your country is an honour every footballer who ever pulled on a pair of boots craves for. It is the supreme accolade, the official recognition that you are the best, or at least among the best, in your own position. But to me playing for Scotland has meant much, much more. It has meant that at last I've been accepted in my own country by my own people.

Leaving Scotland straight from school to go into English football stripped me of any claim to fame north of the border. It left me as an unknown in my own land even when I progressed into United's senior team and was made their skipper. Anyone mentioning that a bloke called Moncur might be worth consideration for the Scottish side was met by an incredulous 'Who the hell is he?' from the fans. They had never heard of me despite my schoolboy and youth caps and one outing at Under-23 level.

I don't kid myself about the reason. It stood out like a beacon. Although I was doing a fair job for my club I still wasn't a big star in England. I wasn't a personality boy like Billy Bremner of Leeds and therefore news didn't filter back over the border.

Ah, you might say, he's cribbing at the old Anglo bit again. He's complaining that if a player is a Scot in England he has to be a genius to make the international team. Well, that's not true although I don't think I'm being controversial when I say that if you play for Rangers or Celtic you have a great chance of getting capped. In fact I'll let you into a secret. If I were a Scottish selector and I was faced with two players for the one position and they were playing equally well I would always plump for the one with the Scottish club ahead of the one in English football. His selection would benefit the League game within Scotland and that must be for the good.

My full international debut came in May, 1968 and looked like a one-game-only call-up to me. Even then I was surprised to get in. I had played against England at Hampden Park in an Under-23 international three months or so before. Instead of being sweeper I was at centre-half marking Martin Chivers and collected a cut head for my pains.

However I mustn't have blotted my copy book for when the full international with Holland in Amsterdam came up I was in the squad. Naturally I was delighted but I still thought I was merely making up the numbers. Celtic's galaxy of stars were not available so someone had to be called in. This time I was moved to my normal position and teamed up with Ron McKinnon of Rangers, the centre-half I've played alongside in all my internationals so far. We got a 0–0 draw but the result was met with some pretty caustic remarks in the Scottish Press. This puzzled and upset me. I felt they were completely unjustified. A lot of people seem to underestimate Dutch football. Don't forget that in the last three seasons two of their clubs have reached the final of the European Cup. Feyenoord won the trophy last year beating Celtic and Ajax lost the 1969 final to A.C. Milan. And as Scotland themselves had lost 3–0 to Holland at Hampden a couple of seasons before I thought our goalless draw away from home more than stood up to the comparison. I hadn't set the world on fire but on the other hand I was content with my performance. No goals conceded always pleases me. It means we defenders must have done our job.

The international, apart from bringing my first major honour, had a more significant bearing on my immediate career. It marked the first real step towards a cartilage operation which loomed ominously before the new season opened and caused me to miss the first round Fairs' Cup tie against (ironically) Feyenoord in the season United won the trophy. I had been bothered by my right knee for some time so that when the inside cartilage twitched during the match but stayed in place I took little notice. But the next morning I was in agony. I could hardly walk. Trainer Johnny Cummings of Hearts, not knowing my history, thought it was ligament trouble and I hobbled back home for a few weeks rest. That obviously eased the situation but only delayed the inevitable.

Although I got through all the pre-season training okay and took part in five-a-sides the first match I played (a friendly against Hibernian in Edinburgh) saw the knee go completely. I'll never forget being carried off by Alec Mutch, our physiotherapist, and little Tommy Robson, our outside-left who was sub that day. Tommy, his face full of concern, was holding the leg in question. Every few steps he would let it drop, then suddenly realize and heave it back up again. It was hell and I was threatening him with everything including murder but Tommy didn't seem to hear a word.

The great pity was that my mother was at the game. She and dad live at Kirkliston just outside of Edinburgh and although he has seen me play all over the place she has always been reluctant to come along in case I am hurt. The sight of me being carried off in obvious pain was too much. She's never watched me play since and even when I turned out in the Fairs' Cup final she travelled from Scotland and looked after our son Paul while dad and Camille went to the match.

The coach journey back to Newcastle from Edinburgh, including a stop for a meal, took four hours during which time I sat with my leg bent and held firmly by splints. But it didn't take Mr Bob Rutherford, one of our directors and a respected surgeon, four minutes to decide it was cartilage trouble. A couple of days later I was in hospital for an operation. The feeling when I woke up from the operation was wonderful. At last my leg was beautiful and straight. After what had seemed an eternity of hobbling around with the leg bent it felt just like getting rid of an itch and was an immense relief.

Although I got straight back into United's side and skippered them to victory in the Fairs' Cup I didn't get back into the Scotland team that season. However towards the end of the season I detected a subtle note of change for the first time. I, previously an unknown, was winning support in the Scottish

Above: That's me kicking clear for Scotland Schoolboys against Wales at Cardiff in 1960. *Below:* I wonder how many big names you can recognise in this Scotland Schoolboys side. Try the front row for a start – from left to right they are Bobby Watson (in track suit), George Moonie, Alex Willoughby, John Markie, George Graham and Ian Mitchell. At the back I'm second from the left and Jim Forrest is fifth

Above: Early days at Gallowgate – and Moncur the apprentice professional helps the groundsmen with the plastic sheets used by manager Charlie Mitten to protect the ground from snow and ice. *Below:* I wish I had this protection every Saturday! I christened this tank the 'Spirit of St James's' for the 15th/19th The King's Royal Hussars after we had won the Fairs Cup

Press for international honours. It even reached the proportions of a campaign after we beat Glasgow Rangers in the Fairs' Cup semi-finals and I got my hat-trick against Ujpest in the final.

Two seasons ago the big breakthrough came. I was in the full Scottish squad all season and played four internationals. But the joy was spliced with sadness . . . immense sadness. We failed to qualify for the World Cup finals in Mexico and I was forced to sit on the substitutes' bench and watch, unable to do a thing to help. The only matches I missed were the important World Cup ones. It was one of the biggest disappointments of my life.

Before the World Cup qualifiers with West Germany and Austria we took on Eire at Dalymount Park. It was September 1969, more than a year after my first cap. Although most of the newspapers thought I had done well enough to clinch my World Cup place the team as a whole took another severe pounding for a sub-standard display. Certainly the Dublin match was hardly the ideal tonic for the immense battles ahead with West Germany in Hamburg the following month and Austria in Vienna in the November.

West Germany, beaten by England in the 1966 World Cup final, were the big obstacle. They were our Becher's Brook. Get over that one and we were home and dry. Fall and we could kiss Mexico goodbye. We simply had to win. Before the match in Hamburg's Volkspark there was a big debate in Scotland about whether I would be in. The Press had played their part in introducing me to the fans back home. To everyone it appeared a clear-cut issue. Ron McKinnon and Billy McNeill to dispute the centre-half role and Pat Stanton and me for the sweeper's job. That's the way I saw it as well.

The real blow came during a training session two days before the game. Manager Bobby Brown called us together and read out the team – and both centre-halves McKinnon and McNeill were in. I wasn't even one of the five subs! Mr Brown was obviously going for experience for a big game and bearing in mind that West Germany included two recognised centre-forwards, Gerd Mueller and Uwe Seeler.

Nevertheless, the selection of McNeill for a role which was really a sweeper's was still startling even to Billy. Full of genuine concern, Billy immediately sought out Pat and I to say: 'I'm sorry. Honestly, I think one of you two lads should be in but I'm a professional and I'm obviously not going to refuse to play.' It was a great gesture by a nice bloke and after our 3–2 defeat McNeill wrote in a Sunday newspaper: 'Scotland slipped up by picking me for a specialist's job. I was almost embarrassed by my selection with Pat Stanton and Bob Moncur in the squad.'

Not being in the side was bad enough but not even being a substitute was a disaster. I felt absolutely sick about it. With no match and virtually no training the whole trip seemed to be a waste. My first reaction was an overwhelming wish for Joe Harvey to phone up and demand my return to Gallowgate. At least I would be busy then. However after the initial shock I learned to take it on the chin but it wasn't easy, believe me. Although I wasn't stripped I sat with the five subs during the game. So did little Tommy McLean, the Kilmarnock winger who was in the same boat as me.

I almost forgot my own frustration when Scotland snatched the lead in an explosive start with a great goal laid on by my room-mate Eddie Gray. The Leeds lad is a marvellous player. He got kicked to bits but he always came back for more. Eddie's goal-tonic wasn't enough, however, and in the end we lost by the odd goal in five amid something of a riot. Tommy Gemmell was sent off in the 80th minute and as he trudged towards our bench the crowd turned nasty hurling insults at the big fella.

It was a long way to the tunnel and the safety of the dressing-rooms so just in case of trouble I decided to walk with big Tam as a sort of bodyguard. Tommy McLean, not knee high to a grasshopper, volunteered to join us and we must have looked a comical sight walking round, two six-footers and a little guy bouncing up and down beside us. The crowd didn't see the funny side, mind you. Without warning the bottles suddenly came flying over. The sky was black with 'em. That's great, I thought. Here's me not even playing and I'm going to get my head split open. Luckily I ducked the bottles with some difficulty but the real gloom was just settling over us like a big, wet blanket. Mexico was now a million lunar miles away.

Defeat left us with only a mathematical chance of qualifying if we beat Austria and West Germany lost their final match against Cyprus. My one consoling thought was that with Mexico now merely a dream the team would probably be changed and I might get a chance in Vienna. Again I was to be disappointed. The Billy McNeill experiment wasn't carried on but Pat Stanton got the sweeper's job. I got the consolation of a substitute's role. I couldn't complain about Pat, of course. Apart from being a first-class player he is a sensible, reliable sort of lad, the type I like very much. In fact we palled up together during the World Cup and shared a room in Vienna.

The lads, still suffering from the memory of Hamburg, lost a poor game 2–0 but Stanton was outstanding, the star man. To me his performance sounded the death knell. I appeared to be farther away from the team than ever. Little did I know that I would be in for the next match to begin a run which was to win me generous praise as the 'find' of the home international tournament!

4 Scotland v. England

Three internationals in a week culminating in an appearance before 134,000 people at Hampden in the greatest match of them all, Scotland *v.* England. That was my unexpected reward for patience in April last year when at last I felt an honest and accepted part of the blue jersey brigade.

It all came at the end of a domestic season which had been relatively impressive without any tangible results. United had given up the Fairs' Cup thanks to an Anderlecht goal cruelly kicked home in the last minute with the full roar of success still reverberating round Gallowgate. In the League we had continued our gentle climb towards the top almost unnoticed. Tenth, ninth and now seventh denoted steady if not spectacular improvement.

Being a defender I took great pride in the fact that we set up a new defensive record at Gallowgate. A mere 35 First Division goals conceded beat the forty-seven-year-old record for a forty-two-match League programme as we know it now. It had been a season concertinaed because of the pressure of the World Cup. It had not affected us but in some cases had led to an undignified scramble to complete the programme and in the case of Leeds United undoubtedly hit their efforts to land the European Cup, First Division championship and F.A. Cup. In the end they got nothing.

A draw with Chelsea in the F.A. Cup final at Wembley meant a replay at Old Trafford and an international ban on players from both sides. That meant Scotland had to operate in the home international championship without players like Billy Bremner, Eddie Gray, Peter Lorimer, Eddie McCreadie and Charlie Cooke. As John Greig and Tommy Gemmell were under suspension for the start of the tournament I knew I must be almost a certainty to face Ireland in Belfast.

Pat Stanton, who had looked to be ahead of me in the race for the sweeper's role, was now needed for midfield. But in the end we even lost him with influenza. That left me the only recognised sweeper in a largely inexperienced squad. Shorn of the big names and with a record of never having beaten Ireland on their own soil in the last twelve years, it was little wonder that the punters plumped for a home win. Yet I am not so sure that our makeshift team wasn't a blessing in disguise to Scotland, a country always noted for the individual brilliance of its stars but rarely for its overall performance as a team.

With new caps John O'Hare, David Hay, Andy Dickson and Willie Carr in the team plus relative newcomers like myself, reputations still had to be made. No one could afford to stand on ceremony, everyone was forced to pull together. This urgency brought us a 1–0 victory with a goal by O'Hare in fifty-eight minutes. A looping cross from Tommy McLean on the right caught out Neill and O'Kane to drop beautifully on to the head of O'Hare who gave Jennings no chance from close in.

One nod of the head brought victory but not the headlines. They were stolen by a man who is a law unto himself – George Best – although this time I'm sure he would have preferred to have remained in the herd. Six minutes after the goal came the incident which knocked everything else off the front pages of the Sunday newspapers. Best was sent off by referee Eric Jennings for 'showing dissent by throwing mud and spitting.'

Every newspaper analysed the Best blow-up in detail and television flashbacks were never-ending but both medias failed to mention or show one significant point: the Scottish player involved in the incident leading to Best's expulsion. It was me! And I must plead guilty straight away by admitting that I fouled George first and he got penalised for retaliating. It was a technical foul, not the sort likely to mame a player, but all the same it was a foul and had the ref spotted it Scotland would have been in trouble.

Before the game it was decided that I should take Best and

McKinnon should deal with Dougan. The idea didn't please me much because Best often withdraws from the front line and I don't like going deep but I was hardly going to argue about my job in the international side. I was only too pleased to be in. During the first twenty minutes I thought we were going to be murdered as Ireland threw everything at us on a muddy pitch but big Ron was handling the Doog well and I felt I was doing as much as could be expected against a player of Best's calibre.

We slowly got a grip of things and after our goal I thought we were on a straight road to victory. Then during an Irish attack the ball was crossed to the near post. Best was just ahead of me as we set off after it and I realised with horror that if I let him go he would get his head to it and probably turn it inside the post. So at the last moment I pulled George's shirt which threw him off balance just long enough to allow my straining, sweat-covered forehead to reach the ball and thump it to safety. My little bit of gamesmanship had occurred on the blindside of the referee but Best, in his annoyance at missing a chance, lashed out with his arm at me and was promptly whistled up for a free-kick against him. Up to that point I felt sorry for the Irishman whose frustration was natural but his resultant behaviour, of course, was completely unnecessary. Virtually every professional footballer has used this foul or suffered from it without losing his head.

The match with Ireland caused something of a flurry in the family. Neither Camille nor my father had seen me play in a full international and on hearing of my selection they hurriedly arranged to fly to Belfast on the morning of the match. Apart from the chance of seeing me they also wanted to see David Craig who was in the Irish team and playing against me for the first time in nearly ten years of soccer together. I was a little apprehensive of clashing with David during the match but fortunately the situation never arose although I must admit that if it had neither of us would have spared the rod!

The Scottish squad was booked to fly out on the eight o'clock night flight but I managed to work a switch with a Press man who was anxious to get home early. He took my place on the eight o'clock and I got his seat on the late plane with Camille and dad. It meant we could all go back to David's house for a party which I must admit held some appeal for me.

That night really rammed home to me what honest, generous people the Irish are. About thirty of us ended up in an out-of-town pub having a sing-song and I was particularly disappointed when it got to ten o'clock and a taxi arrived to take Camille, dad and I the 36 miles to the airport. On arrival I was fumbling about in my pocket sorting out the money to pay the fare when Camille told me that David had already paid but had warned her not to tell me. The ride came to £5 or £6 yet David, after he and his parents had entertained us to a fabulous night, still had to cap it with such a gesture made quietly and without fuss. It typifies one of the nicest lads I know.

Dad, who has been known to take a whisky (!), had been fairly happy at the party and the following morning as I was preparing to play golf he said casually: 'Did I lend you any money last night, Bob?'

'No,' I replied.

'Oh . . .' his voice trailed off. Then he brightened. 'By, it was an expensive night but it was worth it.'

What he was reluctant to mention was that £9 of his money was missing but after he finally admitted it a phone call to David produced the lost notes. The waitress in the pub had found a roll of Scottish notes, guessed what had happened, and had waited for David to claim them. I mention the taxi and lost money incidents merely to show how great the Irish are. They are people who know how to enjoy life and how to make and keep friends, an art which is sometimes lost today.

My Press from the Irish game was favourable and obviously the scribes weren't the only contented people because before we played Wales at Hampden on the Wednesday manager Bobby Brown called McKinnon and I to one side. 'Play as well as you did against Ireland and I won't be calling anyone into the squad for the England game,' he told us quietly. 'You two will get the job again.' It was just a fleeting conversation but to me it meant everything. It inspired confidence and a determination to land the biggest prize a Scot can land – selection to play against England. The fact that the auld enemy were world champions who would be playing their last game before defending their crown in Mexico added extra spice.

I don't know if it was because of Bobby Brown's gesture or not but I've always felt that I had my best game against Wales even though the biggest accolades came three days later. We got a 0–0 draw on a terrible night which wasn't such a bad result remembering that Wales had held England 1–1 at Cardiff and went on to beat Ireland. My personal satisfaction came in bringing off two sliding tackles which, had they failed, would have left the forward clean through to score. I sensed afterwards that those two tackles won me the respect of the more seasoned members of the Scottish squad. In their eyes I had 'arrived'.

Willie Johnston of Rangers slipped his arm round me and grinned cheekily: 'Come to Ibrox sometime and we'll teach you how to really tackle!' It was a light-hearted remark but I felt it held a much deeper significance.

Bobby Brown was as true as his word leaving McKinnon and I together to face England. John Greig had come back against Wales and now Tommy Gemmell joined him for the big 'un. Standing erect in a blue shirt before 134,000 fans during the National Anthem, my mind skipped back over the years to when as a small, chubby-faced youngster I had excitedly elbowed my way into the schoolboys' enclosure to watch Bobby Charlton hit home a scorching volley for England. Then I had prayed that one day I would stand out on the Hampden turf and now I was there. Yet it didn't feel all that awe-inspiring probably because I was too busy thinking of the task ahead. I wasn't in the slightest nervous which, I think, was due to my upbringing in English soccer.

I knew all the England players personally and had faced them scores of times on League grounds throughout England so facing them again wasn't that much different. Had I been a Scottish League player playing against England for the first time I think I might have felt a lot more apprehensive. Throughout the match we were in charge and I felt it was only matter of whether or not we would score. I could never see England winning. The fact that we didn't break the deadlock was partly due to the referee's refusal to give what looked like a legitimate penalty. Colin Stein was tackled almost thigh high in the box and brought down but the referee waved play on. Yet in defence of England I must say that they played well at the back. Although facing constant pressure Gordon Banks was called on to make very few saves mainly because of expert covering by the men in front of him. In many ways England's defensive tactics reminded me of those we adopt at Gallowgate.

I've already mentioned that to me Wales was my best match but this was the one which produced all the adjectives and the shouting. Looking back I still cannot understand why. I felt I did my job adequately but that I did nothing out of the ordinary. In a way the chance wasn't really there to shine with Scotland on the offensive so much. I've tried many times to think of any instance when I got in a real telling tackle or made a border-line clearance and I cannot come up with much. Nothing like the couple of saves the previous Wednesday.

Two words in the Press nearly always sum up my game: reliable or steady. And if I see them I'm content. For that is what I am and what I'm paid to be. I'm not a genius or a flashy player and as a defender I don't want to be. I want to be safe above all else. Yet the fervour raised both in the Scottish and English newspapers after Hampden left me wondering if the reporters had been watching the wrong player. The crowd, too, were very generous. I'm told they gave me a standing ovation as I left the field in a daze with only a few minutes left to play. I say 'I'm told' because I don't really know. I was aware of some clapping but then all injured players receive a sympathetic round of applause as they leave the field. What I was not aware of was the proportion it reached.

Once again reports of an incident involving me were not strictly correct. They stated that I received double vision immediately before I retired after stopping a full-blooded shot from Martin Peters with my face. The truth is that shot never hit my face and I was hurt much earlier, at the start of the second-half to be precise. It occurred when Jeff Astle and I went up for a cross. There is always a bit of jostling when two big fellas go up together and although I got the ball Astle, climbing behind me, accidentally clouted me in the back of the head with his elbow. I felt stunned momentarily but I soon forgot about it as play continued. But after a while an uneasy feeling came back. If the ball was moved quickly I found difficulty in focusing, my vision was blurred, and I was worried about committing a bad error.

Near the end a ball came across the area square and I stretched to get a boot to it. As the ball flew away and I fell I could see it zooming straight into the path of the galloping Peters. I was getting up when Peters hammered a tremendous shot on the run straight at me and I automatically covered up using my hands to protect my face. The ball smashed into my hands and away again and, just as instinctively, I dropped to the ground. I was inside the penalty area and as I had handled the ball, however unintentionally, I had to go down apparently injured as a safeguard against the referee giving a penalty. A professional player worth his salt will always react like lightning to any such situations. As I lay there facing our goal Jim Cruickshank watched the ball cleared upfield before saying: 'Aye, you're all right now,' and I thankfully clambered to my feet.

My eyes were still bothering me and I was shaking my head in an effort to clear my vision. It didn't work so I signalled to the bench that I wanted trainer Tom McNiven on. He decided it wasn't worth risking me for the last few minutes and so I left to sit by the touchline. But the point is whether or not I had stopped that Peters shot I would have come off. It never touched my head and had absolutely nothing to do with my double vision.

I stayed by the touchline until Geoff Hurst scored his offside goal and then decided I'd had enough. A typical West Ham ball to the near post saw Hurst glide home a header which was chalked off but all the same I couldn't stand the tension of watching the dying seconds and I hurriedly made my way to the dressing-rooms. Inside the doctor decided that I should go to hospital for a pre-cautionary X-ray and as the hospital was nearby the doc, Camille and I walked through the crowds to it.

Later I caught a train back to Edinburgh on my way to Kirkliston. It was one of the match specials packed with jostling, arguing fans and I was forced to sit in the corridor. Throughout the journey not one person recognised me as they dissected the game over and over again. I heard my name mentioned once or twice and some doubt was cast on the referee's birth when the penalty decision was brought up but no one even bothered to give me a second glance. I was itching to join in the conversations just for a laugh. Reluctantly I decided against it.

Although we scored only one goal in three matches the series was something of a success for Scotland. We had not conceded a single goal after letting in a hatful the season before and had achieved what Bobby Brown called 'a moral victory' over England. A share of the international championship was ours.

On the playing side there had been several successes one of the most important to my mind being the emergence of two class goalkeepers after years of frustration in this position. Jim Cruickshank's handling of a greasy ball against Wales was immaculate and Bobby Clark proved what I had thought all along: that he is a superb player. He produced the greatest save I have ever seen and I know all about Banks' save from Pele in the World Cup. It was in my first international in Holland. One of the Dutch forwards hit an absolute piledriver that flew past me and I turned round expecting to see Clark picking the ball out of the net. The shot was right in the angle of bar and post but there was Bobby parallel to the bar and only about three feet underneath it pushing the ball round for a corner.

'You should have held that shot, you know,' I told him sternly a little while afterwards.

5 I Skipper my Country

Being made captain of your country in only your sixth international is enough to make anyone blink. Yet it happened to me when Scotland opened their European Nations Cup programme against Denmark at Hampden Park last November. The sixteen-strong squad for the game was due to be announced on the Monday I was flying out with United to Hungary for our Fairs' Cup tie against Pecsi Dozsa. At about the time we were taxiing down the runway at Newcastle Airport Scotland manager Bobby Brown and the selectors were meeting in Glasgow to release the pool.

For the whole of the three days we were behind the Iron Curtain I tried unsuccessfully to find out the names of the sixteen players. I must have asked every journalist in our party to check with their office but they either forgot or communications were so bad it was impossible to hold an ordinary conversation. I felt after my performances in the home international championship that I was pretty certain to be in the sixteen but I still wanted to know what the competition was for the final eleven. And deep down, although I didn't dare think about it, I had a sneaking feeling that I was an outsider for the captaincy.

As soon as I got home from Hungary I dashed to the telephone. Camille had been staying with my mam and dad in Scotland and I knew she would have the pool. Sure enough I was in. And so were Billy Bremner and John Greig. I felt the captaincy would rest between them with me a possible third choice. After all, they had both skippered Scotland before. There was no mention of the captaincy apart from a quote from Bobby Brown saying: 'I've got my man all picked out. I'm going to have a talk with him.' When Bremner pulled out through injury it looked like a straight choice with Greig the favourite.

I had to report to Glasgow on the Sunday after our League game at Southampton which meant I couldn't have been farther away. Arrangements had to be slick because I wanted to spend Saturday night at home in Edinburgh before going through to Glasgow and to do it I pulled out all the stops. It was imperative that I caught the 5.10 train from Southampton – just half an hour after the final whistle. Considering that I had to get bathed and changed in that time it was pushing things a bit so I took all my courage in both hands and asked the police to help. 'Only too pleased,' they said and arranged for a police car to be standing outside The Dell with engine running Hollywood style. I was in and out of the bath almost before I had time to get wet and dived into the car with David Ford, who was going home to Sheffield for the week-end. We zoomed through the streets of Southampton and the crowds leaving the match to make the station just in time. Then at Waterloo a taxi dash got me to Heathrow in time to fly to Edinburgh. In fact I was in Kirkliston long before the rest of the boys were back on Tyneside: their train from London was diverted because of a broken line and it was two o'clock on Sunday morning when they eventually made it!

All Scotland's players congregated at a Glasgow hotel on Sunday lunchtime before going to our headquarters at Largs by coach. Still there was no mention of the final eleven or the captaincy. It was the next day after training that the silence was broken. I was walking downstairs past the manager's room when I was called in.

'I just thought you'd like to know that you will be leading the side out on Wednesday, Bob,' said Mr Brown. My thoughts flashed to the big fella.

'Will you be speaking to John Greig?' I replied.

'Yes, I'll be seeing him and the rest of the players,' Mr Brown assured me.

'Thanks.'

With that the biggest moment of my international career was

over. I was captain of Scotland. In fairness to Greig I must say he was great about it. I had been skipper of United long enough to be neither nervous nor green on the field but there were one or two small points of which I was ignorant. And it was here that John kept me right. For example Scotland's captain always collects money to give to the waitresses who have looked after the team while they have stayed at Largs. John didn't let me forget this small but significant point.

The big thing about captaining Scotland was making sure that I didn't force too much authority on the players too soon. These were men I didn't know too well, not like the players at Gallowgate. I didn't even play regularly against most of them in League matches and one player, Sandy Jardine of Rangers who replaced Bremner, I didn't know at all.

Before the kick-off I received several good luck telegrams and bumped into Joe Harvey, Stan Seymour and Jackie Milburn who had motored up to watch me play – a nice gesture I thought. It was a terrible night with rain pelting down and our display matched it. Although I was quite pleased with my personal performance I was far from happy with the general performance of the team.

We won 1–0 to get us off on the right foot in the Nations Cup tournament but we ought to have won by a hatful. We created scores of chances and squandered 'em all bar one. And even the one we took carried some luck. John O'Hare deceived the goalkeeper by heading strongly downwards instead of for the top corner but even so the ball struck the keeper's legs on the way in. The goal came after only thirteen minutes and even though we didn't score again before half-time I felt we had done a fair job in wearing down the Danes. I honestly believed we would take them in the second-half. We didn't as the Press were quick to point out to me after the game but I was just as quick to remind them that we had collected two valuable points.

I had skippered Scotland to victory and that at least was something to be proud of.

6 How it all Began

I was born on January 19, 1945 into a family already caught up in the thrills and excitement of football. My father had moved to Perth eight years earlier to join the police and one of my earliest recollections is of standing on the touchline in a Balaclava helmet and blue trench coat on an ice-cold day watching him play centre-half for the police team. I remember it so well because at one stage the ball ran out of play and a huge 15 stone Bobby standing near me ran to retrieve it and kicked the ball full into my face. I must have been around four at the time and it was a painful introduction to a wonderful game.

In those days dad, normally placid off the field, had a heck of a temper on it and got his marching orders three times but it was nothing to his younger brother Bert who was twice suspended *sine die*! The first occasion was the result of a tangle with a famous Scottish international. This fella was playing centre-half against Bert's team and was kicking huge lumps out of the little centre-forward. Bert got more and more mad until he couldn't stand it any longer and went up front himself to sort things out. The clash ended in fisticuffs with Bert knocking out the opposing centre-half. When the referee intervened he got thumped as well and Bert got himself a *sine die* suspension. Later he played again under another name and picked up his second suspension for life. The Moncurs certainly made a lasting impression on the game!

It was because of this tendency to flare quickly that my father always impressed on me the need to keep a cool head and, touch wood, it seems to have worked so far. I've never been

Above: It's party time and some of the boys in our promotion side look to be enjoying themselves. That's P.C. John McGrath complete with helmet in the back row. *Below:* The only Newcastle United team to win the F.A. Youth Cup. The side that did it in 1962 is BACK ROW (left to right): Ted Hughes (youth manager), Clive Chapman, Dave Turner, David Craig, Stan Craig, George Watkin, Mattie Gowland, Alan Wilkinson and Benny Craig (coach). FRONT ROW: John Markie, Alan Suddick, Joe Harvey (manager), Colin Clish, Bob Moncur and Les O'Neill

Above: A Bury player is caught with his trousers down – literally – during a League game at Gallowgate. Some of his embarrassed team-mates point to the culprit walking away on the left: Newcastle's Alan Suddick. *Below:* The youngest and the oldest competitor in the 1961 Corporation bowling tournament at Balgreen

sent off and my only two bookings were scratched from the records.

My early football was mainly with the lifeboys in Perth. I attended Caladonian Road School but was too young to play for their team and left a year before I would have been eligible. Like all kids I was mad keen on the game and used to cost mum and dad a fortune to keep me in shoes. Football meant the world, big and exciting, and I used to race down to the local park well before the lifeboys were due to kick off to play my own game.

Once a friend of my father's strolled down early and saw me furiously at it while I was waiting for the rest of the team and the lifeboy leader to turn up. I'd been playing for an hour and a half by the time I proudly donned my sash (we had no strips) and lined up for the proper game. As the ball was centred dad's pal suddenly noticed me jogging up and down on the spot and doing little exercises to warm up. Real professional style it was but hardly necessary after an hour-and-a-half. It became one of the best family jokes.

Only after we moved to Kirkliston to live in 1954 did I make a school side but even then the school wasn't in a league competition and we only played friendlies. However I was about to meet a man who was to have a vital bearing on my career.

Five miles or so up the road from Kirkliston is a small shale-mining town called Winchburgh which has produced such well-known footballers as Willie Thornton (Glasgow Rangers) and Dave Gibson (Leicester). The Protestant and Catholic schools there amalgamated to form a football team to play in the county under-12 league and although I was from Kirkliston I was allowed to join them. Mr Green, the head of the Catholic school, had watched me play in a five-a-side for Kirkliston and I think he had a lot to do with my selection.

Anyway, we got to the final of the County Cup and although we lost by the odd goal we put up a grand performance. The referee that day was Peter Reid, a West Lothian and Scotland selector . . . and the man who was to guide and help me for the rest of my schoolboy career. I didn't know it then but Mr Reid told dad: 'One day your boy will play for Scotland.' He meant the full professional side and not the schoolboys. I only hope he felt some self satisfaction when I did because he helped in so many ways.

At under-12 level I was a goalscoring centre-forward and my hero was Laurie Reilly, or 'last-minute' Reilly as he was known because of his knack of scoring vital goals late in a game.

I used to travel in to Edinburgh to watch Hibernian play as often as my own football would allow. They were a great team then – something like Celtic are today. Remember their forward line? The Famous Five they were called and the names still live on ... Smith, Johnstone, Reilly, Turnbull and Ormond.

After the 11-plus exams I moved to Broxburn High School and directly under the wing of Mr Reid. While there I played for the under 13, 15 and 18 teams and also made the county under-15 team and Scotland schoolboys. I always remember at 13 being picked to play at outside-right for Broxburn's under-18's in the Scottish national schoolboy cup and having my first taste of travelling away and staying overnight. My chance came because the under 15's – my normal side – had lost but the under 18's had drawn with Oban and had to travel for the replay. As the under 15's hadn't a game I was allowed to step up.

We ran raffles to raise the money to travel up the west coast to Oban and, full of apprehension and excitement, we set off by train and stayed overnight in the YMCA. The game itself isn't very clear in my mind except that I was opposed by a giant 6 feet tall full-back who towered menacingly over me. I wasn't very big for my age at this stage and had deserted centre-forward to be shuffled round several positions before settling at left-back where I made the county under-15 side.

Playing directly in front of me for the county was a tall, skinny lad from Lindsay High School, Bathgate. His name: Tommy Gibb, who is now my team-mate at Gallowgate. Also in the side were centre-half John Markie from Bathgate St

Mary's and the Broxburn keeper Cliff Ewington. Both Markie and Ewington were to play for Scotland schoolboys with me and join United as apprentice professionals.

I have already mentioned the debt I owe to Mr Reid, who got me into the county side and showed such tremendous dedication to his work. I have often marvelled at the unquenchable enthusiasm of men like Mr Reid, amateurs who are prepared to give unlimited time and energy for nothing in return except the pleasure of seeing raw material turn into gold. That enthusiasm was never shown more clearly than the day Broxburn were due to play Linlithgow in an under-15 match. Fog caused the referee to postpone the game but Peter Reid wasn't to be beaten. Three of us were considered good enough to play for the under-18's and as they had a match 35 miles away Mr Reid decided to rush us there. It cost him £13 out of his own pocket to hire a Bentley to get us to the game in time but he did it without a second thought. To him the effort and cost were well worth while.

League football was still a long way from my mind although I loved the game but I was to be forcibly reminded that the time was drawing near when I had to make a decision on my future. That reminder came with the Scottish international trials late in February, 1960.

Four teams were selected to play two games at Stenhousemuir and I was to turn out in the first. Outside-right against me was a youngster called William Morgan who was later to be transferred from Burnley to Manchester United for £90,000 but I felt I did well against him and after the match I was approached by a man who pressed a bit of paper into my hand. On it was written: 'George Bargh, scout of Preston North End.' I had received my first approach. Mr Bargh asked if he could see my father and I told him he was in the stand. He explained to dad that Jimmy Scott, Preston's chief scout in Scotland, was ill or he would have been there himself but added that in any case Preston were very keen for me to go to Deepdale.

My father didn't want to know. At least not at that time.

He was more concerned with me completing my studies and if possible making the Scotland schoolboy side. The scouts had to wait a little longer.

I played in two more trials before the team for the first international of the season was picked. At Bo'ness the selectors were unable to part the twenty-two lads and decided to arrange one more game before committing themselves. So we had to go through all the agony of anticipation again at Linlithgow. Then came the moment of truth. And I was in!

On a Friday night, March 18, 1960 in heavy rain and on a filthy, gluepot of a pitch I proudly pulled a blue jersey over my head and went out to play for Scotland.

We were playing Ireland at Grosvenor Park, the home of Distillery and looking back the Scotland team that night makes very interesting reading. The forward line, for example, all later made the big time. It read George Moonie (Rangers), Alec Willoughby (Rangers), Jim Forrest (Rangers and Aberdeen), George Graham (Arsenal) and Ian Mitchell, now at Newcastle. Willie Morgan, my opponent in the trials, couldn't get in and never did that season. Behind the star-studded attack I formed a full-back partnership with John Markie. Cliff Ewington didn't keep goal because of injury but he came into the team later. The attack did its job okay knocking in three goals but we defenders let in four to get us off to a bad start in Scotland's jubilee year.

However I still kept my place and went on to collect five caps which is more than the usual season's quota. I was lucky in as much as we played a couple of extra games apart from our Victory Shield matches, one against England and one against West Germany. We lost twice to England and once to Ireland but beat Wales and West Germany.

Dad has always been one to horde my clippings and sometimes when I go back home I can get a kick out of sifting through them and letting the memories flood back. Especially the early clippings about schools football. For example, the London *Evening Standard* brought out a souvenir edition before we played England in a show match at Wembley ... my first appearance on the hallowed turf in front of 90,000 spectators made up mainly of schoolboys armed with tuck boxes and bottles of pop.

In the pen pictures on the back page it said 'Robert Moncur: Good kick in both feet. Has a good positional sense, tackles well and used the ball intelligently. Always cool.' The perfect player at 15, eh? Pen pictures in newspapers and club programmes never fail to make me laugh. Nearly always they fall into the 'two good feet and strong in the air' category regardless of who they are talking about.

We got thumped 5–3 at Wembley but the scoreline doesn't tell the full story by far. In fifty-three minutes we were five down and after Willoughby had pulled a goal back we lost our goalkeeper, Ewington. But we kept going and got a couple more goals. By the end it was England who were hanging on. Despite the scoreline I was delighted with my personal performance especially when I got home and read the complimentary reports in the newspapers.

Under a photograph of me smiling all over my face in the *Edinburgh Evening Dispatch* I read: 'Hewitt raced through the Scottish defence for what looked like a certain goal but Broxburn High's Robert Moncur at left-back made a great tackle to clear.' Then further on it said: 'Moncur again saved Scotland from a dangerous position when he cleared the ball from Thwaites who was making straight for goal.' My, it felt good.

But soccer doesn't allow you to stay on cloud nine for long. In the return match with England at Pittordrie I came back down to earth with a bump. This was to decide the Victory Shield and I was moved to centre-half to skipper the side. After Wembley we were all determined to put one over on England and we swept into a seventh minute lead through George Graham, who cracked a screamer from 25 yards into the net. Before half-time we had missed a penalty and as England equalised on the resumption it proved a costly boob. But my real anguish was still to come. In sixty-five minutes I messed about on the edge of the penalty area – an unforgiveable sin in soccer – and lost possession for England to pinch the winner.

So instead of reading words of praise in the Sunday papers I had to put up with vivid descriptions of my mistake which all agreed had spoilt an otherwise good display. It was my first lesson in how cruel soccer can be – and how stupid it is to try and be clever in a defensive position. Ever since I've had little time for frills round the penalty area.

I was learning the game match by match and against West Germany there was one move which brought a feeling of immense satisfaction. A ball struck firmly and sharply across goal headed straight for me by the post. It was travelling at a fair lick but I was able to judge it perfectly and at the last moment I dummied a German forward by opening my legs and letting it whip through for a goalkick. That wasn't a risk but a carefully worked-out piece of soccer planning. It represented my first professional move in the game and pleased me no end. We beat West Germany 2–1 in the first-ever schoolboy international between the two countries.

During the Scotland games the interest of the scouts in me really hotted up. I (or should I say my parents) were subjected to the sort of persuasion and high-powered sales talk that can easily leave you flummoxed and bamboozled and that is why I'll be eternally grateful to my father for handling things so well. It was his calm influence that finally got me going in big-time soccer.

7 Why I Chose Newcastle

I turned down two of the greatest managers in the game to sign for Newcastle United. Back in 1960 the great supremos of soccer were Manchester United's Matt Busby and Stan Cullis of Wolves. Both were revered, even worshipped, by people inside and outside the profession. They were the heads of two massive empires . . . men with immense power who usually only had to beckon with their little finger and players ran to join them. Yet I, a mere schoolboy, rejected both Manchester United and Wolves to go to Newcastle, the last club in the queue. Why? What made me turn my back on all the glamour at the top of the tree?

The answer, in a nutshell, is that Old Trafford and Molineux lacked something that Newcastle United had in abundance: homeliness. And that's vitally important to a kid about to go out into the big wide world on his own for the first time. I felt like a little boy lost on my two visits to Old Trafford. The super stars were there all right but the place was cold and impersonal and I thought it lacked a little discipline although I must say that I had – and still have – an immense respect for the man who took me there, chief scout Joe Armstrong. Matt Busby has said a lot of kind things about me since. He picked me out as a future star when I played at Old Trafford as a centre-half in the Central League and tipped me as Scotland's next captain before I really broke into the international side.

Stan Cullis, too, was just as much of a gentleman. When I signed for Newcastle he wrote to me wishing me all the best. It wasn't a type-written letter either. It was in his own handwriting – a personal touch I appreciated.

Remember I told you how the mad scramble all started with

Preston North End leading the field. George Bargh, their scout, saw dad after the international trial at Stenhousemuir and in the first full match against Ireland Joe Armstrong made his move. But throughout all the proceedings my father played it strictly fair. First in first served and that meant Preston was to be my first port of call.

Scouting is a highly competitive field and the tricks scouts get up to in an effort to steal a march are quite amusing. Shortly after the first two approaches I was due to play for Scotland against England in a showpiece match at Wembley. And Preston laid on the works for my mother and father. A train down to London, hotel, tickets for the match and a night out at the London Palladium to see Liberace. They lived like royalty for the week-end.

However Manchester United weren't to be outdone. When mum and dad boarded the train at Edinburgh's Waverley Street Station who should happen to be aboard but Joe Armstrong. He sat with them throughout the journey drinking tea and coffee as my father played his cards cautiously. Joe wanted both of them to be *his* guests for the match but of course dad couldn't change his arrangements.

That summer was hell for me. I lived out of a suitcase as I travelled England having a succession of trials. As time wore on I hated it and became heartily sick of football. I longed to go back home and forget about trains and digs and more trains. I had a fortnight at Preston, then managed by Cliff Britton, a fortnight at Manchester United, a week-end at Wolves and another visit to Old Trafford. And all the time other clubs were pressing dad for a spot on my summer timetable. Jock Stein's brother made an approach on behalf of Burnley and Newcastle United entered the race late through their scout Peter Nellies.

The first time I did well at Manchester United and they wanted me to sign straight away but dad had promised other clubs that I would be visiting them and so I agreed to return later. When I did I was pretty sick, didn't impress half as much, and was thankful to leave.

Stan Cullis also wrote to dad after my visit there asking me to go back again but I never did. The nomad was ready to quit. Back at home dad had a long talk to me about all the clubs involved. The name of Newcastle United cropped up again as Nellies had now become pretty persistent and dad knew Tyneside a little. As a laddie he had spent a few holidays at South Shields and used to go to St James's one week and Roker the next. Would I mind a look at the place? It would be the last. I agreed and dad phoned Nellies to tell him the news. He was through to our house like a shot and bright and early on the Monday morning I was on yet another train heading back over the border.

The following day I played in a practice match at half-back and that night when dad went to meet the train from Newcastle I wasn't on it. They had asked me to stay until the Saturday and I agreed. During the week Charlie Mitten, then boss at Newcastle, asked me: 'What foot do you kick with, son?'

'It's six and two threes,' I replied.

'Right, you'll play at inside-left at West Wylam on Saturday.'

So inside-left I was and I thumped in four goals to really set people wondering. My future on Tyneside was almost assured. This was definitely the club for me. Everyone was so friendly and genuine. They were really interested in you as a person. Whereas before I had the feeling of being just a number this was different. Alan Thompson, in charge of Newcastle's Juniors, and Ted Hughes, manager, showed an immediate interest in my progress. And to top things off my pals from the Scotland schoolboy team, John Markie and Cliff Ewington, were on the staff. I was put into digs at Whitley Bay with them. Other youngsters like David Craig, fresh over from Ireland, were just as friendly. This was great.

Ted Hughes wrote to my father inviting him down to look over the place. My father readily agreed and when he arrived he wandered on to the Gallowgate terracing. A full-scale practice match was in progress. He stood watching it for twenty minutes or so until the ball ran out near him and Jimmy Scoular went to get it. Then dad asked if he could have a word with Charlie Mitten. Scoular, friendly and helpful, called over the boss.

Dad introduced himself and asked where I was. Confined to digs with a cold, came the reply. So dad quickly set off for Whitley Bay where he found I'd gone to the pictures! I'm afraid youthful devilment was still in me then.

However once he had dug me out it didn't take long to convince him that Newcastle was the place for me. I had already signed amateur forms but on October 22, 1960 I became an apprentice professional to end my few months of globe-trotting. My father had steered me through everything well.

Of course wherever I went I was bound to feel homesick at times. And it happened at Newcastle. Luckily I had someone to help me through those early teething problems: someone who has since become a very close friend. I refer to Alan Thompson. A young lad fresh from home needs personal attention. A guiding hand if you like. Alan provided it. In fact he did an awful lot in keeping me at Newcastle. I didn't stay long in my Whitley Bay digs before moving to fresh ones in Two Ball Lonnen in the west end of the city and Alan was a constant visitor.

He loved golf and as I was a 22-handicap beginner he was around every Sunday morning to take me to Alnmouth for a round. Every young footballer will agree that Sunday is the worst day of the week when you're away from home. Every morning during the week you are training and on a Saturday you're playing but Sunday – that's a long and lonely day. So Alan's golf outings were a welcome relief. Now Alan is living next door to me in Crawcrook and still providing me with a golfing partner.

8 Early Days under Mitten

Charlie Mitten was a man who courted controversy. One of soccer's characters, stories of his reign at Gallowgate still circulate around town. They still cause a chortle and I don't think Charlie would mind. He seemed to like the publicity that he attracted.

You've all heard the best ones I suppose. Like the day Charlie brought in one of his greyhounds – he was mad keen on the sport – and Len White had to nip off the treatment table so that the dog could have a spell under the heat lamp. I was in the boot room cleaning the boots when Charlie walked through with the dog.

It was headline time when Charlie was around Gallowgate but I'll tell you one thing: for me he was great. You must speak as you find and both as a man and a manager I found Charlie Mitten the tops. He was a tracksuit manager with a load of new ideas and a special interest in his youngsters.

We got bags of attention and tips from him and the utmost consideration. All those who lived away like myself were sent home once a month all expenses paid. It was Charlie who insisted upon that. Every practice game he stripped off and played himself. Furthermore he was the best left winger we had on the books. He had been a star with Manchester United and his skill still shone through. Many a first-team defender got a skinning from the boss.

Charlie was a man with a sharp brain and he was always coming up with new ideas. Some were sound, sensible and winners. Others were wildly outrageous and flamboyant. All made people sit back and take notice. For years United's strips had been traditional – black and white stripes, black shorts and black stockings. He changed all that. Every team under his command got a new rig-out. The black pants got a white band round the bottom and the stockings were changed to white with black and white striped tops. Those pants caused a right commotion. Everywhere United played the wags in the crowd had a go.

'Your slip's showing, Scoular,' they would yell at Jimmy, one of the toughest men in soccer.

And when the team ran out it wasn't to booing or clapping. It was to wolf whistles.

Another of Mitten's ideas was putting polythene sheets on the pitch as a protection. It used to be row upon row of burning braziers to melt the snow and ice or loads of straw. But Charlie wanted polythene sheets: huge, long strips the length of the field. As one of the groundstaff boys, it was my job to help to lay them. And what a job. Air bubbles used to get underneath which made it very difficult to pin 'em down. Then trying to remove them on a Saturday morning with a ton of snow on top took superhuman strength. One day we didn't pin them down properly and when we came in the next morning after a strong overnight wind we found half the sheets on the roofs of the Leazes houses! But what killed the idea once and for all was the time we covered three-quarters of the ground on a Thursday afternoon. By the Saturday there had been a thaw and the quarter of the ground we hadn't touched was perfect while the three-quarters that had been covered was brick hard and icy.

Those days as an apprentice pro were great fun. We used to give poor Arthur Charlton, the groundsman, a terrible time. After training late in the week, he was in charge of us when we were given such chores as laying the polythene and sweeping the stand and terracing in readiness for Saturday's match. It never went smoothly because we all used to like to rag Arthur but the afternoon we went on strike nearly caused him to burst a blood vessel. I should explain that the apprentices used to split into two groups: the Geordies who were, of course, the local lads, and the Rebels, who were the Scots and Irish lads. This Friday afternoon we hadn't swept the stand out before an important League match. Suddenly Arthur appeared on the scene, his face red and his temper high. 'Get hold of those bloody brushes and get up in the stand,' he bellowed. There were only the 'rebels' around so we went looking for the Geordies – and found them singing in the bath! They didn't want to know about any more work. And as it was a good hour's stint we didn't fancy doing it either while the rest of the lads trotted off home. So we told Arthur where he could stick his brushes. Poor bloke. He suddenly realised he had trouble on his hands and time was running out. A filthy stand on match day and *he* had questions to answer. All his anger drained away as he almost went on his knees to get us to do the job.

Mitten's era saw me grow up with some of the really big names in United's history. At the time I was learning the game the top men were Jimmy Scoular, Bob Stokoe, Bobby Mitchell, Ronnie Simpson, Alf McMichael, Ivor Allchurch, Dick Keith and Len White. Several had a profound bearing on my early education in one way or another and I should like to give particular mention to three of them – Scoular, Allchurch and Stokoe.

Scoular, that hunk of Scottish granite, was club captain at the time. He had skippered United in the 1955 F.A. Cup final when his brilliant crossfield passing to Mitchell had demoralised Manchester City. Relatively quiet off the field, his tongue on it almost matched the ferociousness of his tackling. That tongue was to bite deeply into me and leave its mark. My dressing-down came during a five-a-side when I was playing in Scoular's team and did something stupid. He waded into me with a mouthful that was enough to make my hair stand on end. I was completely taken-aback. Never before had another player spoken to me like that, not even a senior one. And there were no apologies from Scoular afterwards. It was a sharp reminder that professional football is a man's game and if you are to enter the jungle you must live by its laws. There is no easy passage.

I've often thought about the Scoular incident since I became United's skipper. On occasions I've lashed the youngsters in the same way. Whether they think of me as a so-and-so or take it as justified criticism I don't know but what I do know is that it bothers me a little. In fact, I must admit that because I can remember Jimmy's lashing so vividly I have been known to explain to the apprentices afterwards that my outbursts in the heat of a game shouldn't be taken personally but as a sort of advice. The kid glove treatment is no preparation for the years ahead.

Scoular, of course, could be as nice as the next man. He had a bit of a reputation locally as a player of bowls and although it's not a popular game among footballers I was quite a dab hand myself. I had learned the game as a 13-year-old back in Kirkliston when I used to go along with my mate Stewart Meikle and help the greenkeeper at a private bowling green. It got into my blood and I had a go myself. Eventually Stewart used to partner me in tournaments.

After joining United I entered the Leith open singles on a visit home during the summer. Scoular used to live at Livingstone not far from Edinburgh and he was up visiting as well. So he came along to see me play in the semi-finals. I felt quite proud when the club skipper shook me by the hand and wished me all the best. Only trouble was I went on to lose!

Allchurch, like Scoular, was an artist on the field. The Golden Boy of Wales they used to call him and how right they were. He was the inside-forward supreme. It was not usual for young pro's to get to know the seniors very well, of course, but I got close to Ivor simply because he was a great pal of Alan Thompson. Ivor, a quiet man with an uncanny knack on the dart's board, taught me how to shield the ball. He was a master at it and he came back to the ground a few afternoons to pass on his skills.

Another friend of Alan's was Bob Stokoe who sometimes used to play golf at Foxton Hall with us. A deep thinker and very dedicated, Stokoe hates to lose whether it be at golf or football or anything else. It sticks in his throat. Bob is still a close mate of mine and he is one of the few people in the game I would consult if I had a problem I wanted to take outside the club. Two others are Stan Anderson and Jimmy Greenhalgh, now in partnership at Middlesbrough but once our skipper and coach respectively.

Impatience marked my early days at Gallowgate. When I was in the Newcastle's juniors I wanted to be in the seniors and when I made it I was restless again after a few weeks. I kept thinking I wasn't progressing rapidly enough. An inability to wait is a natural trait in a teenager, I know, but with me it reached serious proportions. At times I thought I would never make it and if dad had given me the slightest encouragement I would have been up the road home like a rocket. This had nothing to do with my earlier bouts of homesickness or with the club itself. This was merely dissatisfaction with myself and my progress.

I suppose a lot of people looking back shudder at periods in their life, usually early on, when they almost blew their career. I shudder when I remember my attitude in those early times. When I said homesickness no longer came into it there were a couple of reasons why. One, as I've explained, is that Alan Thompson helped me so much and the other is the digs I got. They were first-class. Funnily enough I had two landladies before I got married and both were called Mrs Johnson. And both lived within a stone's throw of each other. I spent a year with the first Mrs J. in Two Ball Lonnen and then moved round the corner to my second Mrs J.

Digs are very important to the unmarried footballer. The landlady virtually becomes your second mother and her responsibility is great. Seeing you get the right food and keep the right hours are just two of her jobs. Fish and chips and bed in the early hours of the morning after visiting clubs are no good to kids. The second Mrs Johnson, who had me for most of my footballing life as a single lad, was so conscientious that she wouldn't go to bed at night until all 'her boys' were in.

People like that are worth their weight in gold to a football club.

Alan Thompson, Mrs Johnson, my father . . . they all helped to keep me going in the right direction when I was at my most vulnerable as a kid. To them I say thanks.

Above: Soccer American-style. Newcastle train among the skyscrapers of Chicago during last year's tour. *Below:* Here I am indulging in my favourite pastime with Bobby Mitchell, Gordon Marshall and Stan Anderson

Above: Are our hopes going up in smoke or is it a celebration? I light huge cigars for David Ford, Bryan Robson, Iam McFaul, and John Cowan during a Fairs Cup trip to the Continent. *Below:* The tension is off – temporarily – and Newcastle's players relax round the swimming pool at our hotel in Estoril. Left to right are David Craig, me, Iam McFaul, Ollie Burton, Jim Scott and Graham Winstanley

9 We Win the Youth Cup

When I scored a hat-trick in the European Fairs' Cup final someone asked me what it felt like to score goals worth thousands of pounds. 'Just the same as normal,' I said deadpan. 'All my goals are precious – you see I keep 'em specially for cup finals!' The poor bloke didn't know whether I was serious or not and excused himself looking flustered and embarrassed. I bet he'll never ask me another question like that. I was referring, tongue in cheek, to my last goal of any real note . . . in the F.A. Youth Cup final seven years before.

The laugh is I couldn't get my place in the junior side at half-back and so I was shoved into the attack to add a little height, weight and robustness to a smallish front line. It worked, too, although I didn't kid myself I was another Mannion or Carter.

In the final we held Wolves to a 1–1 draw at Molineux and in the Gallowgate return on May 2, 1962 before 20,000 spectators we won 1–0. But it wasn't the left foot that did the trick for me then. It was my head. From a corner taken by Les O'Neill to the near post I managed to beat the defence and head home . . . an exact replica of a goal I had scored in the Central League the previous Saturday.

Remember the team which brought United their first Youth Cup success? I wonder how many you can name now. The final side was Stan Craig; David Craig, Clish; Chapman, Markie, Turner; Gowland, Suddick, Watkin, Moncur and O'Neill. Outside-right Alan Wilkinson was injured in an early round and didn't play in the tournament again. Only David Craig and I are still at Gallowgate although several others have enjoyed successful careers elsewhere.

Alan Suddick, back in the First Division last season with Blackpool, is the biggest name but what about Dave Turner (Brighton skipper), Colin Clish (Rotherham and Doncaster), John Markie (Falkirk) and Les O'Neill (Darlington and Bradford City)? Suddy was the star of the side, of course. Though still only 17 he had already appeared in the League team and was bursting with potential. To me it has always been one of the tragedies of the game that Alan didn't fulfil his potential and become not only a full international but one of the greats.

He had as much natural ability as George Best when he was a kid and he played just as effortlessly. He would work a ball and shoot as though we were playing in a five-a-side on the car park. A lot of people used to say that Suddy was a big head but that wasn't true. It was merely that he had so much ability and liked to display it like a new toy. His talent fizzled out a little because of his love of life and impishness but he's a lot more mature now and I believe he is at last gaining the one thing he lacked – consistency.

Alan was always the practical joker, the sort of lad who would delight in creeping up behind you, tapping you on the left shoulder and then nipping smartly to the right. It could be absolutely infuriating at times but one look at the grin splitting his face and I couldn't help but laugh. Often he couldn't control his joking even when on the field. I always remember in a Second Division match against Bury at the park, Newcastle were awarded a free-kick just outside the area. Bury's defenders quickly formed a wall and began pointing and gesticulating at each other as we prepared to take the kick. The serious expressions on their faces proved too much for Suddy. He nipped smartly behind the wall and pulled down the shorts of one of the Bury players. The lads could hardly take the kick for laughing.

Others in the Youth Cup team like Colin Clish, the skipper, and Dave Turner, who held my proper position at left-half, were much more serious than Suddy. Clish, a cultured sort of footballer, never used to swear. He might shout 'ooh, you bugs' after taking a particularly nasty rap on the shin but he would never forget himself completely. His seriousness and his constructive approach to the game brought me a laugh the following season when most of us had stepped up into the reserves. Joe Richardson was then in charge of the Central League side and Joe as you will probably remember, was never the most scientific of full-backs in his day. He was more of a sleeves-up type and proud of it. Anyway at the usual team talk Joe, addressing Clish, said impassively: 'Whatever you do get the ball up the field.'

Colin, looking obviously affronted at this uncultured approach, protested: 'But if we boot the ball up the field it'll come straight back.'

'Then boot the —— back up again,' growled Joe.

Some time afterwards when the tactical boom was about to explode upon us the boss arranged for the first team and reserves to play Burnley in pre-season friendlies to try out a revolutionary new 4–2–4 plan. The seniors did pretty well getting a 1–1 draw at Gallowgate but we got hammered 6–0 at Turf Moor.

On the following Monday morning we all met at our Hunters Moor training ground to compare notes. Jimmy Greenhalgh, the senior coach, produced a rosy report and then turned to Joe.

'How did it go for you,' Joe?' he asked.

'Well, all I've got to say is that it was like being attacked by bloody Indians,' snorted Joe. 'They came at us in droves. It was three against one, four against two and five against three.'

His feet were going on the spot forty to the dozen to indicate attacking Indians.

'As far as I'm concerned you can stick it,' he finished defiantly. The room was in an uproar.

Yet under that bluff exterior Joe Richardson was a shrewd judge of a player. He could spot potential and was never afraid to back up his opinions openly.

My introduction to the Youth Cup side was against Manchester United at Old Trafford and I got off the mark by scoring our first goal in a 2–1 win. Suddy got the other. It gave me a great deal of pleasure because not only were Manchester United one of the country's most famous nursery sides but they were also the club I nearly joined. However I must admit that my goal was somewhat lucky. O'Neill, a cocky little character who floored us the first time we saw him by turning up in a Teddy Boy suit, was in a spot of bother near the corner flag and I yelled to him as I ran up in support. He pushed the ball back and I decided to drive it first time across the face of the goal. Imagine my surprise, then, when the ball flashed into the net. I didn't tell anyone I hadn't meant it, of course. That was a big night for us. We stayed overnight in the Queens Hotel in the centre of town and were given ten bob each spending money by director Stan Seymour.

After that we beat the likes of North Shields before getting to the crunch, the two-legged semi-final and final against Portsmouth and Wolves respectively. The first leg of the semi at Fratton Park almost saw us play without a goalkeeper after a right giggle which finished with big Stan Craig getting three stitches in his rear end! The trouble began when Dave Turner decided to scramble two pears on the train journey to London. Fourteen of us crammed into one compartment like big, hungry bears waiting to be thrown a bun. Up went the first one and there was a mad scramble before one of the lads emerged triumphant clutching a squelchy pear. That meant there was only one left and determination was increased. Thirteen pairs of hands were at the ready as Dave prepared to release the prize. Up it spun and with elbows thrashing we all made a dive forward until a piercing scream stopped us in our tracks. We turned round following the direction of the noise and gulped. There was Stan Craig, all 13½ stone of him, sitting with his backside hanging out of the window – and we were passing through a station!

'Get me off, get me off,' he yelled but no one heard him as tears of mirth rolled down our cheeks and we all dashed back to our carriages at the approaching footsteps of coach Benny Craig. David Craig helped Benny to lift a bleeding Stan from the glass which was shattered like a spider's web and when we got to London Benny had to take Stan to hospital while we continued our journey to Portsmouth. That night while we were getting a ticking off from Ted Hughes, a schoolmaster in charge of the party, for giggling at the façade poor Stan was having three stitches put in his back end. But it was British Rail who had the last laugh. They sent the club a bill for £10 for the damaged window! Stan, suitably patched up and reluctant to sit down at half-time, played against Portsmouth the next day when Pompey won 1–0 with a lucky goal.

Virtually every team that wins a trophy has a match where near disaster turns into glorious triumph and ours came in the return with Pompey on a night of torrential rain. One goal down on aggregate didn't appear too bad with home advantage to come but within five minutes of the kick-off things looked about as cheery as a coalmine at midnight. A corner found our defence half asleep and East, their centre-forward, promptly smacked home a rebound.

Half-time came with us still incredibly two down on aggregate despite laying seige to the Pompey goal but we finally got a break in fifty-eight minutes when O'Neill netted a fine, low shot from a Turner cross. However, as in all good stories the heart-stopping went on. Portsmouth hauled themselves back to a 3–1 overall lead when our vulnerability to a corner was exposed again for East to rocket a grand header home. With less than half an hour left things were dodgy but a sudden goal surge saw us power to a 4–2 win to go through to the final on a 4–3 aggregate. The goals came from Gowland (68), O'Neill (75) and Watkin (85) with me having a hand in the late clincher. I nodded on a Chapman ball for Watkin to stride forward and chip the ball over a despairing keeper.

A double meeting with the cubs of Wolves stirred up tremendous interest both in the North-East and the Midlands. A crowd of 14,000 watched the Molineux first leg with 20,000 at Gallowgate for the return. I know a lot of Second Division clubs today who would like those sort of gates for their senior team. Wolves, under Stan Cullis, had a lot of bright kids and were firm favourites to win the trophy. Several of them have since hit the jackpot. There was Bobby Thomson and Peter Knowles, both future England Under-23 internationals; Ken Knighton, a left-half later with Preston; centre-forward John Galley of Rotherham and Bristol City; and goalkeeper John Barron of Nottingham Forest.

After Wolves had grabbed the lead through Galley on the half hour we got a 1–1 draw which delighted us with a superb goal from little Clive Chapman in fifty-three minutes. Clive had been dazed in the first-half after a sickening collision with Knighton but he shrugged it off to daze Wolves with a cracking equaliser. The little guy was always the greatest with the ball in front of him and I can still see him running from the half-way line to within 18 yards of goal to lash a tremendous left-footer high into the net. Three times on the way Chapman emerged from blockbuster tackles with the ball to the growing admiration of the crowd. The way he would meet a challenge from much bigger and more brawny players was a lesson which I quickly learned. Both David Craig and I often use the same method now. When a player came directly for him Chapman would bend his left leg under him and shoot out his right stiffly behind the ball. There is nothing stronger than a leg held rigidly straight and inevitably the opponent, running into the ball with a foot wedged directly behind it, would cart-wheel over the top. Three players went the same journey on that particular run at Molineux.

A week after our draw with Wolves I signed full-time professional for United – on April 24, 1962. So my winning goal in the return was something of a celebration, I suppose.

Although Charlie Mitten had more or less built the side we actually won the cup during the brief reign of Norman Smith. But by the time the following season had begun a third manager was in charge at Gallowgate . . . a manager who was to have a profound influence on my future. His name: Joe Harvey.

10 My Debut – and then Promotion

My League debut came towards the end of my first season under the boss. I had made the Reserves pretty regularly but as a wing-half or occasionally a centre-half and not at inside-forward as in the Youth Cup. Late in the March of 1963 United, with promotion hopes still flickering, were due to visit Luton Town, bottom of the Second Division and looking relegation certainties.

Big John McGrath was injured and as John Markie was also unfit I had been at No. 5 in the Central League team for the last three games in which we had won two and drawn the other, all away from home. I was training with the seniors at the time and therefore it wasn't too much of a surprise when I was told to pack my bags and catch the five o'clock train to London. Even so at the tender age of 18 I still sat with a knotted feeling in my stomach as the train pounded towards the capital.

Outside the Kenilworth ground I bumped into an old pal of mine from Kirkliston, Freddie Jardine. Although Freddie is a little older than me we had grown up together and battled through many an 'international' in the backstreets around our home. He was now a full-back with Luton but wasn't playing that day because of injury. As we chatted Freddie helpfully ran through the Luton forward line for me giving me one or two tips. Although I was up against a tall centre-forward called Goldie it was the inside-right who occupied most of his time. The inside-right's name was Ron Davies . . . the same fella who now terrorises defences in a Southampton shirt!

'Watch him,' said Freddie. 'His favourite trick is to race towards the moving ball at full speed and then dummy to let it run through his legs.'

It proved sound advice for within a couple of minutes Davies did just that. But instead of being caught as I almost certainly would have been without Freddie's warning I merely stood behind Ron and collected the ball as it came through his legs. Even though Ron didn't enjoy the greatest of games overall he still showed that uncanny goalscoring knack by knocking in a couple of good 'uns. It kept the score down to 3–2 although we should have won by a mile. My handling of Goldie received lavish praise in most quarters but I suspect that the adjectives were trotted out mainly because an 18-year-old debutant had finished up in a winning team away from home.

The real margin of our win is shown by the fact that Barrie Thomas and Ron McGarry finished as passengers and Dave Hilley had blood pouring from a nasty gash in his leg. We were two up in less than an hour thanks to Thomas and Jimmy Fell and approaching the last five minutes led 2–1. When Suddick chipped home a beauty it looked as though the margin was going to be more in keeping with the run of play but a minute from the end Davies pulled back another goal.

Because the occasion obviously has sentimental memories for me I would like to recall Newcastle's team. It was Hollins; McKinney, Dalton; Neale, Moncur, Iley; Suddick, Hilley, Thomas, McGarry and Fell. I managed two more League games before the end of the season both away, to Charlton and Rotherham.

The Charlton game, which we won 2–1, was on a Tuesday night and we caught the sleeper back to Newcastle getting in at 7.30 in the morning. Two hours later while the rest of the seniors were tucked up in bed at home I was back on another train out of the Central Station for Manchester to defend the Youth Cup.

We were to play Manchester United at Old Trafford again in the fourth round but this time there was a significant difference. Our cup-winning side had been torn apart because of age with only John Markie and I remaining and we were well and truly thumped 3–0. A young Irishman called George Best was on the Manchester left wing and a match report in a local paper recorded that 'Best beat his man magnificently to get in a low, hard cross that brought the first goal.' Also in the Manchester side, I remember, were David Sadler, Bobby Noble and Willie Anderson, who was later transferred to Aston Villa.

We didn't manage promotion that season or the next when my development continued with three more Second Division outings all at centre-half early in the season. At this stage no thought had been given to me playing sweeper or back man of the back four – the role I have now and prefer to any other. My present sort of game hadn't really become commonplace in the mid-60s but I believe it has greatly benefited defences and centre-halves in particular since. The front man (i.e., the older type centre-half) can now go to meet any dangerous ball with complete authority and confidence knowing for certain that there is someone behind him should he miss. There is no longer any need to dither or hold off. The centre-half is now the man to commit himself and go for the kill and the sweeper or cover man is the reader of the game waiting for the break.

Season 1963–64, which brought me three more League games as I've already said, wasn't a particularly happy one for United. We finished a moderate eighth in the table while arch rivals Sunderland were promoted along with Leeds United. To make things even worse Bedford Town, a non-league side, came to Gallowgate in the third round of the F.A. Cup and won 2–1. We felt the shock waves throughout the club for weeks afterwards.

But that season marked the beginning of a new era for the club although it wasn't perhaps immediately realized. Stan Anderson was bought from Sunderland half-way through it and made skipper and David Craig and Frank Clark emerged as first-team full-backs by the end.

Anderson made a tremendous difference to youngsters like myself, Craig and Clark. A deep thinker, Stan liked nothing better than to 'talk' soccer with anyone who would listen and his knowledge was such that he found a ready audience with the younger lads on the books. It was nice to find a senior pro willing to give us so much time. Stan was the first man to tell me straight to my face that my main qualities made me a defensive player.

The dark, cultured Anderson was king of the attacking wing-halves, a player with a silk-smooth Rolls engine in him, but he told me earnestly: 'Don't be fooled into copying me, Bob. Going forward's not for you. All your strength lies in playing at the back reading the game and blocking the holes. Develop your game on those lines.'

Later Joe Harvey told me exactly the same thing but at the time I took little heed of Stan on this particular point. I liked going forward when at wing-half and I felt I could do it well enough. By the time August came round the Bedford blues were just a bad memory. We were ready for the off even though Alan Suddick was to miss the start of the season after a cartilage operation. Eventual success, I think, often depends on getting off to a flying start and Newcastle achieved their object with five wins and a draw in the first seven games. We never looked back after that and from mid-October we remained in a promotion place to finish up as Second Division champions.

A lot of credit for promotion has since been given to the half-back line of Anderson, McGrath and Iley, rated by top judges as the best to wear United's colours for some time. They were magnificent – there's no doubting that – and the contribution of those two stylish wing-halves Anderson and Iley is shown by the fact that they notched 13 goals between them.

As you can imagine it was pretty frustrating for me trying to break through against those three. I had no chance of replacing any of them on merit so it was merely a matter of waiting for an opportunity through injury or a tactical reshuffle. As Anderson played 41 League games, McGrath 42 and Iley 38 it was almost a complete shut-out but I still managed to sneak in 11 appearances. They were all early on long before the exciting run-in (my last appearance was in November) and all at left-half. I played in two bursts, the first a four-match stretch when Iley was injured and then a seven-game run which began when Ron McGarry was suspended and Iley moved to inside-left.

In fact the whole defence during 1964–65 picked itself. Big Gordon Marshall was ever-present in goal, David Craig only missed two games and Frank Clark none. The rapid strides made by Craigy and Clark in their first full season were particularly impressive.

David, who joined the club so long ago with me, has developed into the best full-back in Britain. I say that unhesitantly and I know there are a lot about like England's Keith Newton, Tommy Wright and Terry Cooper, big Tommy Gemmell in Scotland, and Peter Rodrigues of Wales. He has never looked anything but class from the day he walked into St James's Park and the only person who didn't realise it was David himself. For a long time he didn't feel good enough which was exactly the opposite attitude to the one I adopted. I've never been as classy as Craig but I've always thought that if you didn't openly support yourself no one else would. David was far too quiet and reserved for his own good.

The dream of First Division football again on Tyneside was finally realised on April 16, four matches from the end of the season, when United beat Bolton 2–0 before a worshipping 59,960 crowd at Gallowgate to make sure of going up. The championship was clinched later on. I was one of the 59,000 squashed into Gallowgate like sardines in a tin. From a spot in the paddock just to the right of the tunnel I cheered myself hoarse as the boys roared to victory with a goal in each half from Jim Iley and Willie Penman. Everyone had palpitations early on as big Wyn Davies, then playing for Bolton, climbed unbelievable heights to rattle the woodwork with bullet headers but Wyn's efforts finally brought him an injury which reduced his effectiveness. Still, I'm sure his form that day did a lot towards bringing him to Tyneside the following year.

At the end of the match I was still pinned in the paddock as the boys emerged in the directors' box just above me to give the crowd a victory salute. Suddenly their shirts were peeled off and came fluttering down into the crowd to begin the biggest stampede since the gold rush. As I stood there watching my mates like Craig, Clark and Robson receive a deafening ovation I never thought that the next time Gallowgate saw such a scene I would be standing beside them leading the crowd in singing after winning the European Fairs' Cup. Funny, isn't it? One of the crowd one day and one of the heroes the next. That is what makes soccer so extremely exciting.

At the end of the season fifteen of us embarked on a short tour of Denmark and West Germany as a celebration after four years in the Second Division wilderness. We played five games in twelve days winning four and drawing the other but as with all tours the real memories have little to do with the actual playing side. The mood was already light-hearted after gaining promotion and we treated the tour more as a working holiday than anything else.

On the first night in Horsens we all went out for a few lagers and it soon turned into a light-hearted party. Clarky had taken his guitar on the trip and before long he was entertaining us with a few of his songs. He's a pretty good singer is Frank and the boys, who were used to his performances, gave perfect order as he sang 'I'm nobody's child', a sad ballad. You could hear a pin drop – except for the loud guffawing of Jimmy Greenhalgh, our coach. The noise cut through the air like a hot knife through butter and completely drowned poor Frank. It was a party, after all, and Jimmy couldn't understand why we were all so quiet listening to a solemn song. In the end Frank, battling against the tidal wave, couldn't stand it any longer. He thumped down his guitar and walked out threatening never to air his tonsils in public again. The place was in an uproar! Now Frank laughs at it but at the time he was genuinely furious and looking back I suppose it is easy to see why.

I was still one of the young fellas in the team then and I'd got all dressed up in my best suit for the first night out with the boys. Really it was not how much I drank (it was only lager anyway) but more the intoxicating mood of revelry and the late hour, but by the time I tottered up to my room that night I was completely exhausted. All I wanted to do was go to sleep and I think I must have opened the door and flopped into bed in one movement. Anyway, the next morning when I woke up I was curled up like a kitten . . . still in my brand new suit! It was like a dish rag.

Big Gordon Marshall (our goalkeeper) was sharing the room with me and I immediately moaned to him about allowing me to go to sleep without undressing. Marsh, a big, amiable guy who smokes a pipe, murmured in that soft Scottish brogue of his: 'Aye, Bob, you looked so comfortable when I came in I didn't like to disturb you, laddie.' I could have crowned him!

During our stay in Horsens we were told that we were going to be taken on a coach trip to one of the local beauty spots. From all accounts it was a millionaires' playground and we were all looking forward eagerly to the visit. Eventually after an hour or so in the coach we arrived at a tatty old harbour on a lake. All there was to be seen were a couple of boats with paint flaking from them and an old fish-cutting place. We were so amazed we couldn't speak.

As we all clambered off the coach not knowing where to go or what to do the Churchillian voice of William McKeag boomed out sarconically: 'Boys, don't go on ALL the roundabouts!' Mr McKeag, a man with a rapier wit, had done it again. Dave Hilley, in front of me, doubled up with laughter and we all followed suit.

If ever a man can produce the perfect phrase for the occasion it is Mr McKeag, a club director who has been Lord Mayor of Newcastle, an M.P. and a solicitor among a million other things. Anyone dismissing him lightly as I unfortunately did on our first meeting is in big trouble. The first time I met him he asked me a question and I replied quickly without thinking. It's the worst thing I could have done. Immediately I was pinned in the corner . . . I was in the dock. 'Tell me,' said Mr McKeag with heavy emphasis, '*why* did you say that?' Boy, was I sweating by the time I eventually got away. Now I weigh up my answers very carefully whenever Mr McKeag's around. I've seen too many flighty young players cut down in mid air by the wily Mr McKeag just as I was.

From Horsens we nipped over the border into Germany for three games before returning to wind up the tour. It was in Wolfsburg, the home of the Volkswagen, that Bill Thompson showed us his versatility after we had visited the car factory in boiling heat.

We all went out for a quiet night but to our horror we found that the local restaurant cum bar we had 'adopted' didn't boast a chef. And we were all very, very hungry. It looked like a major crisis until Bill, built like a barn door, suggested that he had the answer. If the manager was agreeable he would serve us himself. Before long Bill, complete in apron, was installed in the kitchen and steak sandwiches were coming out thick and fast.

Big Bill from Bedlington was quite a character. On the field this massive centre-half with the deep-set eyes and the style of a runaway steam-roller was a fearsome sight. But off it he was as friendly and helpful as they come. Apart from being emergency chef Bill acted as our valet on the tour. Often just before we were due to leave for a match Bill would be carefully pressing a pair of trousers for one of the boys. If any job had to be done we only had to send for Big Bill.

I've told you earlier how helpful Stan Anderson was to us kids with his advice and theories on the game. Well, the same night as Bill served us steak Stan served me with so much advice that we both got lost! Near the end of the night I slipped downstairs to the toilet. A few seconds later Stan appeared and promptly started an earnest conversation on my game. It must have been an hour before we surfaced again ... and by this time the place was in darkness. Everyone had gone home. Although we managed to get out of the restaurant we were lost. We hadn't a clue where we were. In actual fact the restaurant was only 200 yards from our hotel but we didn't know it and blithely walked two miles in the wrong direction still deeply engrossed in the rights and wrongs of football before someone put us on the right road.

Stan's complete dedication in guiding the young had given me a chuckle a few days before. This time Bryan Robson was the lad in the corner on the end of a lecture. Absent-mindedly as he talked, Stan would dump his long cigar in the ash tray until the end sprayed out like an umbrella and then seconds later he would attempt to smoke it again puffing furiously as he spit the words out of the side of his mouth and jabbed Pop continuously in the chest with the forefinger of his other hand. With the broken cigar protruding from his mouth it looked for all the world as though he'd walked straight into a brick wall.

The tour was completed in Aalborg where in a ceremony full of pomp and dignity we were all initiated into the Guild of King Christian IV in the wine cellars of the 17th century Jens Bang mansion. I should explain that the guild was formed during the occupation of Denmark in 1942 as a retreat for the Danes and the last British people initiated before us were Princess Margaret and the Earl of Snowdon. Officials of the guild wearing scarlet robes solemnly read out the rules of membership while we agreed to obey them and washed down our promises with mead.

At the end of the initiation we lined up crocodile style with our left hand on the right shoulder of the person in front and followed two banner carriers round the mansion chanting a song which was totally incomprehensible. Any minute I expected someone to leap out and tell us we were on Candid Camera!

All this qualified us for a King Christian roll of honour and a large key to the mansion. The funny part was some of the rules we had to obey and which were meticulously written out on the roll. One said: 'Any man seducing another man's wife must buy a round of mead.' There were also penalties to pay for burping and spitting on the floor!

Life was very, very sweet and easy to live after the years of drudgery in the Second Division.

11 I want to leave United

Two seasons in the top flight and elation turned to frustration . . . at least for me. In fact I got so depressed that I was determined to leave Gallowgate and but for the matter of £5,000 (not a big sum in soccer's transfer market) I would have been a Norwich City player by now and probably buried for ever in East Anglia.

But let's not jump the gun. If I may I would like to fill you in with the background to a move which I thank God never reached completion. Our first season back in the premier division – 1965–66 – brought me 19 games and a First Division debut against my old foes Manchester United at Old Trafford. Now most players have their 'favourite' team, a side they like playing against more than any other. Mainly it's a club which for some reason not quite apparent they always do well against and on occasions it's a club they were once with or might have joined. Manchester United are that sort of club to me. I've always had an urge to show them my best face since those trial days at Old Trafford and as I'm the type of player who reacts automatically to the big occasion (and believe me appearing before the Stratford Enders is certainly that) some of my best reports have been against the famous Reds.

The Manchester United forward line back in 1965 was John Connelly, Bobby Charlton, David Herd, Denis Law and George Best so my introduction was expected to be a hot 'un. I was centre-half in between the promotion heroes Anderson and Iley and Ollie Burton was emergency right-back. Yet against all the odds we got a 1–1 draw and almost did the impossible by winning. Nobby Stiles snatched the equaliser five minutes

Above: A moment of personal triumph and elation. I wheel round with my arm in the air after scoring the first goal of my hat-trick against Ujpest Dozsa in the 1969 European Fairs Cup final. *Right:* We are back at Newcastle Airport with the Fairs Cup after our triumph in Budapest and all hands want to touch the treasured trophy

Later at St James's Park it's the same old story as the boss shows off the cup to the crowd

from time with a lucky shot from 20 yards that struck Burton to change course in mid flight.

A brown-stained scrap of paper which records the merit marks for the match is still one of my proud possessions. It shows that Moncur got 10 out of 10 but in truth the real hero was the guy who shared maximum marks with me, goalkeeper Gordon Marshall. Big Marsh was magnificent as he was regularly for us around that time. In fact the following season he saved us from relegation and so put us on the road that eventually led to Europe.

The boss has always reckoned that the second season after promotion is the dangerous one. First time emotion and the crowd sweep you to safety but next time round, with everything bedded down, it's often a matter of fighting for your life. So it proved at Gallowgate. We eventually finished third from bottom after looking certainties for the big drop around Christmas. In the end we fought with the strength and desperation of a dying man to haul ourselves to safety but it was a mighty close call.

After my Manchester United 'flyer' things didn't exactly hum along for me. I felt I was beginning to stagnate for the first time in my career and that season of fighting against the relegation tide drove home the point in the cruellest possible way. Although I played a few extra games this time I still couldn't get a regular place in a struggling side. I was shuttled from left-half to centre-half and on to right-half and even finished up over Easter at right-back. I had more ups and downs than a yo-yo. From one week to the next I hadn't the faintest idea what position I would be playing or even if I would be in the team.

By now I was 22 years old and felt that I should be becoming established as a first-team regular if I was going to make it at all. A footballer's career is short and too much time cannot be wasted in 'coming through'. To make matters even more urgent I was due to get married during the summer (June, 1967) and wanted to buy my own house. That meant I must be sure about my future and I wasn't.

The obvious thing to do under the circumstances was to seek an interview with the boss to clear up one or two points and that is what I did. I told him I needed security especially now I was getting married and that, as I felt United couldn't give it to me, I was ready to leave. The boss was quiet. He let me have my say. And when it became apparent that I was determined to go in an effort to get a regular first-team place he agreed although somewhat reluctantly.

I was referred to the chairman, Lord Westwood, for the rubber stamp to a move and he told me: 'As you want to go, Bob, and you've been a good servant we will do all we can to help you.' My days at Gallowgate appeared numbered and I sat back to await developments. They weren't long in happening. Norwich City and Brighton appeared on the scene together. Both wanted me but they went about their business in different ways. Brighton manager Archie Macauley asked if he could talk to me before talking cash with United. The boss agreed. But Norwich manager Lol Morgan used the more orthodox approach by trying to iron out the fee first.

I wasn't really interested in Brighton. They were a Third Division club and I thought I could do better than drop two divisions. I also knew through the newspapers of Norwich's interest and they looked a much better proposition. However I still talked to Mr Macauley on the phone. He told me he wanted me as a centre-half and asked me to visit Brighton for a look round. I never went.

Instead I followed the Norwich business in the newspapers. I had already made up my mind that once the clubs agreed I would sign providing my wages were reasonable. I wouldn't want the earth only security and peace of mind. United, it seemed, were asking £25,000 for me which I thought was reasonable enough but evidently Norwich didn't. They looked upon Joe Harvey as some sort of Dick Turpin. 'I didn't know Joe Harvey was a poker player,' said Lol Morgan in the Press. 'He must be, judging from the price he is asking for Moncur. I'll be calling Joe's bluff.' To Norwich I wasn't worth £25,000 even though I was only 22 with a fair bit of First Division experience. Such a thought wasn't very comforting, I can tell you.

Every day I seemed to read that the boss was holding Norwich to ransom and that Norwich wouldn't cough up. They were true to their word, too, for although I learned later that they would have gone to £20,000 for me they were not prepared to put down an extra £5,000 and eventually the whole thing fizzled out. I have often wondered what Norwich felt the following season when I not only got my cherished wish of regular first-team football but was also made skipper!

Norwich's carefulness with money could be one of the reasons why they are no more than an average Second Division club. Not long afterwards they could have signed Bryan Robson but once again they kept a tight grip on the purse strings and the deal fell through. Every time Pop hits a goal now it must make them wince.

By the time the Norwich saga was over the new season had crept up on me almost unnoticed and I was thrown into the frenzied activity of twice-a-day training. I hadn't much time to think about anything else. The start for me was as inconspicuous as could be expected for a player who had almost been transferred. For the first seven games the nearest I got was a seat on the substitute's bench a couple of times without being called upon.

The team played unchanged during that time but the results were not all that good and finally a 4–0 tousing at Nottingham Forest brought wholesale changes at the back. Iam McFaul, David Craig, Ron Guthrie and I were brought in to face Coventry City at Gallowgate. Within no space of time we found ourselves two goals down and in real trouble. Coventry weren't an outstanding team then which made things even worse. But to our credit we pulled back to 2–2 before half-time and went on to snatch the winner in the second-half. As I had made the vital third goal I was happy enough with my performance.

Imagine my shock, then, when the team sheet was pinned up for Sheffield United a few days later and I was dropped.

The fact that one or two others were keeping me company was no consolation at all. I was seething and I stormed along the corridor to the boss's office looking for a row. Jim Scott, who had also been axed, was standing outside waiting to air his grievances. 'Do you mind if I go in first, Jim?' I said. 'This won't take a couple of minutes.'

An hour and a half later I emerged to be met by a grinning Scotty. He swept my apologies to one side saying: 'Think nothing of it – listening to you two through the door was like a pantomime.' Then as he opened the door for his session he added: 'Let me know when you're going in the next time – I wouldn't miss it for the world!'

The set-to with the boss was the worst I've ever had. I told him point blank never to pick me for the first team again unless he was going to give me a chance. It was like opening the floodgates and letting everything come tumbling out. The more I talked – or rather shouted – the more I could feel my anger being drained away to be replaced by a feeling of satisfaction. At least I had made my feelings clear.

The Bramall Lane match brought a 2–1 defeat with wee Willie Carlin, 5 ft. 3 in. in his stockinged feet, heading the winner against the challenge of three six-footers, Marshall, McNamee and McGrath, who had gone on as substitute.

More soul-searching was to follow and the following Friday during a practice match the boss strolled casually across to where I was standing. 'I suppose I'll have to play you again tomorrow,' he said nonchalantly. 'I told you you'd be back, didn't I?' He turned on his heel and walked away leaving me gaping at the coolness of the man. It was Arsenal at home on the Saturday and we won a brilliant match 2–1 with a superb header from Wyn Davies in the dying minutes. Wyn climbed almost as high as the pylons to head home a corner. Although I didn't realise it at the time I had turned the corner at last. From that day to this I have never ever been dropped.

I played every game to the end of that season, helped United to qualify for Europe for the first time in their history, skippered the side when Jim Iley was out, and picked up Scottish caps at

Under 23 and full level. No wonder I'll never forget Saturday, September 30, 1967 . . . the day it all began for me.

The return with Arsenal at Highbury months later was, in a way, equally significant. It was the first time I ever skippered United and it brought a moment of terrible embarrassment with my mate, Frank Clark. Iley was out of the side and on the train journey to London the day before the game we were all ribbing Clarky, who was looked upon as stand-in captain. I was doing my fair share which was to make things worse later on.

The big shock came at the team meeting held in the Great Northern Hotel at King's Cross before we took the coach across to Highbury. The boss started off by saying: 'You'll be taking the ball out today, Bob,' and then ploughed straight into the tactics without another word on the subject. My head was swimming. I looked across the room at Frank, wondering desperately what was going through his mind. I knew he would be disappointed. But, worse still, I wondered if he thought I had known what was to come.

For once I never concentrated on the tactical talk. All I wanted was for the ground to swallow me up. Frank was more than a colleague he was a pal and somehow the trick seemed a dirty one although it was all very, very innocent. I didn't speak to Frank on the matter until we were in the dressing-room getting changed. Then I quietly tried to explain that I knew nothing about the choice – it was as much of a shock to me as it was to him. Really I shouldn't have worried knowing Frank as I do. He took it magnificently, told me to forget all about it and wished me all the best. Since then he's been a tremendous help to me in my job as skipper both on and off the field.

We got a 0–0 draw that day which was something of an achievement considering our patched-up side. Wyn Davies, Albert Bennett, Jim Iley and John McNamee were all missing through injuries. Alan Foggon, only 17, and Tot Winstanley (19) were making their League debuts and John McGrath was playing his first League game for five months. He had a blinder, too, but it was to be his last in a black-and-white shirt. Unknown to him Southampton boss Ted Bates was in the stand and talks had been opened on his transfer before we boarded the train back home.

It was the following season, 1968–69, when I became regular skipper once I had overcome my cartilage operation early on. I missed both the opening Fairs' Cup ties against Feyenoord when Frank took United into battle but I was fit and back from the second round right up to winning the cup.

With my new job came a growing awareness of a new responsibility . . . something which I take very seriously these days. Often the job and the attitude that goes with it are misunderstood. That is why I want to deal with being skipper in some depth. I want for once to give my side of the story.

12 Responsibility

There is much more to being captain than tossing the coin or clapping your hands and shouting and bawling at your team-mates.

Newcastle United is right at the heart of the city. Rightly or wrongly it affects thousands of lives every day. Trade from the little corner shop outside the ground to the chain stores lining Northumberland Street can be affected by what happens inside St James's Park. So being captain of Newcastle United is at once a great honour and a great responsibility.

As leader of a bunch of young men continually in the public eye it is necessary to be very careful about what image is presented to the world. Dress, appearance, manner immediately become important. One slip and it reflects throughout the team and the club. At functions whether it be a rotary club or a school prize-giving you are no longer representing merely yourself. You are Newcastle United and as such must produce the right balance between dignity and friendliness. It is not being big-headed to think of yourself as Newcastle United. It is being honest, frighteningly honest. You are the official representative of the club and must not let it down.

This is where Camille comes in. Not only is she an understanding wife – and she has to be with me out at functions so much – but she is always ready to make sure that every little thing is right. That I don't boob in any way. She even keeps a diary of my engagements and helps answer any letters. That is what I call a real wife and it is no coincidence that things have gone right for me from the day I got married.

Being captain makes a man a bit of a loner inside the club. I sometimes do something the players don't understand. Once or twice I have had to make unpopular decisions. I might say unpopular things on the pitch. Sometimes I say to myself: 'You shouldn't have said it like that,' or 'that was a bit rough.' But I just can't say to myself, 'You shouldn't hurt his feelings.' Football is a very hard game and the man who can't take some physical or verbal hammer won't last long. It is part of experience.

What players often don't understand is that I must back the boss up to the hilt whether I agree with him or not. It's part of my job. I'm the bridge between him and the players. I can argue with him in private and put my point of view as forcibly as I can but once the decision has been made I must transmit it to the rest of the boys as gospel. I have to make it sound right.

Team selection is another point. I've heard it said that I pick the team. That's rubbish. Only one man picks the team at Gallowgate: Joe Harvey. No one else. He may talk to me about it in the same way as he talks to the coach Dave Smith but when it comes to the crunch it's the boss who locks himself away and produces the team sheet. He listens to advice and opinions but naturally does not always accept them.

What put the stupid idea round that I had something to do with team selection was an incident in Lisbon during our Fairs' Cup-winning season. Unfortunately it got into the Press and a few of the players didn't like it. The team had been announced to the Press a few hours before the kick-off with Dave Elliott in instead of Ollie Burton. I was sitting by the swimming pool with the boss when he told me about it. He asked what I thought. And I told him. I said that for this particular match and this particular job I would prefer Burton. It was nothing personal against Dave. He is a fine player and a nice lad. It was just the personal opinion of a professional and was meant to be taken as such. The boss obviously thought about it. Perhaps he asked others for their opinion. Perhaps the torrential rain which suddenly swept the Portuguese capital had something to do with it. Anyway, he played Burton and we got a result.

What made me fuming was that a Sunday paper carried the story of my talk with the boss. It made it appear as though I virtually selected the side. I knew what Dave Elliott must have thought. And I was sorry. Very sorry. But I couldn't apologise. I had done my job honestly and quietly as I believed I should do it. I had taken responsibility. After all, it wasn't me who leaked the story to the Press.

Occasionally I am aware when I walk into a room that the lads have suddenly dried up. It makes me smile inwardly. Although they probably don't believe it, I can understand their attitude. I may be one of them in a way but I still represent authority and that makes it difficult. Some probably think I'm a big-head. It's bound to happen. And I don't pretend to like it. But I am not going to chuck the job or lose a night's sleep over it. They will sometimes say things like, 'You'll be all right – you're a pal of the skipper's.' That's silly. I would never let friendship colour a professional opinion. I would never be able to live with myself if I did.

One of the most difficult problems facing a skipper is knowing when to take up a player's cause. One or two want me to be spokesman for things which are none of my business: things they should do themselves. For example I cannot speak on cash or contracts. It is up to the individual to fight his own fight there. I don't know their personal terms or want to.

By and large, of course, the boys realise the responsibility I feel and accept it and even help me. People like Frank Clark and others are invaluable to me both on the field and off. Whether it be advice with tactics during a game or a willingness to shoulder some of the burden of official functions they can always be called upon to rally round. United are lucky that way. Overall we have a great bunch of lads and the team spirit for which the club is renowned reflects this.

The great difference between me now and as a young player is that a young player is almost wholly concerned with his own performance. Now I worry about the whole team. I worry like mad about the results. One of the reasons why United have progressed as a team is that all the senior players feel the same way. They are more concerned about Newcastle United than themselves – or at least as much concerned and that is saying a lot because no man is more proud than a professional footballer. They all want to look good. The attitude of one for all and all for the club is vital and is probably the result of our increasing experience, our maturing and our getting to know each other better every day and every match.

Of one thing I am abundantly certain. For all its responsibilities, for all its worries, for all its problems I am the proudest Scot south of the border for I am captain of Newcastle United in a city in which they really know what football is all about.

13 That Man Harvey

I'll always remember Joe Harvey's one-sentence summing up of football. 'They've got the ball, you want it, so you go and take it.'

Perhaps it's an over simplification but it portrays the man perfectly. It is down to earth, sincere, direct and honest. So is the boss, or 'the gaffa' as we sometimes call him. He is a man as rich as the earth under the plough but with a subtleness which is at first surprising.

I know it is a common pastime around town to call him Lucky Joe and too-easily dismiss his achievements because he is basically a homely man instead of a tyrant or a high-faluting waffler. But such talk is foolhardy. No one could be so lucky so regularly over such a long period of time. Soccer isn't generous: it's cruel and honours are won the hard way. If Joe Harvey hung every medal he had ever won at Gallowgate on a watch chain his stomach wouldn't be big enough to take 'em all!

As a player, he skippered United to promotion in 1948 and two F.A. Cup final victories in 1951 and 1952. Three years later he was coach when the silver pot came to Tyneside again and when he returned as manager it was to shoot United to the Second Division championship in 1965 and the European Fairs' Cup at the first attempt in 1969. That's as impressive a roll of honour as you will find and there isn't a single blemish on it anywhere.

Lucky? My foot. It's just that some people cannot believe (or don't want to believe) that success can come to nice guys. I can vouch for his success as a manager. I know of it first hand. From the inside. And from the scores of football people I have talked to he MUST have been a great skipper.

Mind you, he must have been a bit of a tartar as well. The sergeant major type if you like. Ida, his wife, tells me she used to line up the kids when he came home and say: 'Right, here's your dad. Give him a salute.' But he's mellowed now although he'll still have a go if necessary. Even at the younger players though perhaps not so hard at a sensitive one. The great thing is that even if you are at the wrong end of a rollicking you know there will be no hard feelings afterwards. And that's a great quality to have. Don't get the idea that Joe Harvey is like a bull at a gate. He has a great sense of humour. He can be subtle and tactful too. He doesn't pay attention to frivolous gossip. He knows his players and he has his own unobtrusive ways of finding out if a player has a problem. There's no song and dance about it.

Like most managers he gets phone calls, mostly anonymous, claiming that Joe Bloggs was in the Dirty Duck on Friday night swigging back pints and had to be helped into his car. Mainly the calls come after a defeat. But the boss doesn't go off the handle. As a former player he knows the penalties which have to be paid and he doesn't take any action without concrete evidence.

Joe is a man's man and he treats his players as men. I remember the first time I met him. He wasn't the boss then. I knew him only as an ex-player but his friendliness struck me right away. I went into his shop on the West Road with Alan Thompson for some sweets after a Sunday golfing session. He talked easily about the game. Wanted to know if I liked it at Newcastle. If I had good digs. I thought: 'This is a homely fella who talks my language.' Some time later I met him again at Goswick Golf Club near Berwick. I'd gone with my father for a game of golf and he was playing with Alan. We shook hands.

It was that summer Joe Harvey was appointed manager of United. Dad's reaction was that he was a good type, down to earth. But Alan warned me with a grin: 'He is a real tough character. Watch 'im.' It didn't take me long to find out Alan was right. The first time Joe joined us on the car park for a five-a-side we clashed. The boss emerged in an immaculate maroon track suit and played on the opposite side to me. In a jostle for the ball I suddenly got a jab in the mouth from Joe's elbow. It hurt too. Right, I thought, wait till the next time. I'll get you. Back came the boss loving every minute of it. As he elbowed past I gave him a little nudge. Down he went with his ankle buckling under him. 'That'll keep you quiet,' I said triumphantly. The ankle went up like a balloon. It should have been in plaster but the boss wouldn't agree to that. He wouldn't give in. But all the same he was hobbling for about six weeks and he's never joined in the five-a-sides since. He confines himself to head tennis now and cheats like mad.

The boss is golf daft like me. He's a good player and, just as in football, he hates to lose. It goes against the grain. That was plainly obvious in our first game and if Alan, my partner, hadn't given me the nod I think I would have been decapitated. We were playing at Ravensworth and I was holing everything despite the bumpy greens. I'd had about three single putts and we were four up as we approached the sixth green. As I was lining up to win the hole with a birdie the boss growled: 'Look, Moncur, if you hole this putt I'll show my bare backside round this golf course.'

I was 15 yards from the hole and would have been happy to get down in two but I rapped the ball without much thought and it bobbled, kicked and flew straight into the hole. I was about to say: 'Howway, get your trousers off,' when I spotted Alan out of the corner of my eye nodding his head from side to side. Biting my tongue just in time, I watched the boss stride across to the next tee seething with anger.

In later years Alan and the boss were playing Ken Harvey and me at Ravensworth again in an old 'uns *v.* young un's match. Ken, Joe's son, is a great golfer – he's a former professional – and we were going like a bomb. To add a bit of spice to the game we were playing for sixpence a birdie and we were about eight birdies up. The boss was getting a bit vicious with Alan when suddenly there was a roll of thunder and a flash of lightning. Joe's face brightened immediately. 'That's it,' he said. 'We can't play in lightning,' and promptly walked off the green. We've never been paid to this day.

I've had a lot more serious set-to's with the boss than that, of course. We were always arguing about something. But can you tell me of anyone interested in football, inside or outside the game itself, who isn't always arguing about it? I told you earlier about the trouble after he dropped me a few seasons ago. That was only one occasion. On another I got into a row bang in the middle of a derby match with Sunderland before 57,600 spectators at Gallowgate.

It was back in 1966–67, the season we almost went down. We had just lost 6–0 at Blackpool and bought Wyn Davies in midweek. That had inspired interest on Tyneside but although Wyn had a good debut we were getting well beaten 3–0. And I wasn't exactly having a blinder.

In those days substitutes were only allowed for injured players. The boss decided I was injured. I had to come off. He passed the message to me through our skipper Jim Iley. I said get knotted – or words to that effect. I played on, keeping my eyes away from the trainer's dug-out. The boss was fuming and when I went to see him on the Monday he let me have it. I'd disobeyed orders by not coming off and I got it in the neck. Valiantly I stuck to my guns. 'Would *you* have come off?' I asked accusingly. 'Of course I would,' he growled. 'Any good professional would have. There's your reputation to think of, you young whippersnapper.'

For the next two or three weeks after that I never played anywhere. Not even in the reserves. I cooled my heels doing nothing. And the lesson was rammed home. No one disobeys the boss. I've watched it since . . . but I haven't been put to the test again. I've never been brought off and substituted so I don't know how I would feel the next time.

Not that I want to find out, mind you!

I don't trust the boss! . . .

14 America and Canada

The New World . . . it sounds grand, doesn't it? In May last year we sampled life on the other side of the pond during a four week tour of America and Canada arranged to help promote football (sorry, soccer!) out there.

After piloting round Europe on very serious business for two years the idea of taking things easy and enjoying the most modern, jet-set way of life appealed enormously. Six nice little friendlies against local opposition finishing with a showpiece match against German cracks Eintracht Frankfurt sounded cosy and not too taxing.

Sixteen of us were making the trip – Wyn Davies, Frank Clark and David Ford were all missing because of injuries – and it took us eighteen hours from leaving Newcastle Airport to touching down in Chicago for our first game. Starting by going east to get west didn't help, of course. We flew to Amsterdam and from there took the long hop to Toronto and then over the border to Chicago.

We were booked into the Ramada Inn, downtown Chicago and I was soon introduced to life American-style. A motorway swept like a silver ribbon past our hotel and into the distance and the first night I was woken up at 5 a.m. by a tremendous noise. It was as though the whole world was blaring car horns angrily and continually. Sleepy-eyed I staggered out of bed and over to the window to pull back the curtains . . . and there was a traffic jam as far as I could see. At five o'clock in the morning it was ridiculous. I had to nip myself to make sure I had really woken up.

Later that day we trained on a local park amid the mighty skyscrapers of Capone-land and I had my first encounter with the American Press. And what an encounter. It started well enough. A smart young girl introduced herself as Lynda Morstadt of *Chicago Today* and asked for an interview. I was only too pleased to oblige – after all, we were there to promote the game and publicity was as good a way as any. It was soon obvious that she had no idea what soccer was all about but we ploughed on and at the end I said goodbye and wondered exactly what I had let myself in for. When I found out I could have died.

Alongside a photograph of Pop Robson and David Craig training on the local park with a caption reading, 'English soccer players practice move called heading,' was a four-column headline screaming, 'Moncur is one for the birds.' I blinked and felt my blood suddenly run cold. What an introduction to a tour! In the article I was compared to 'Broadway' Joe Namath, the American football star whose performances off the field equalled those on it.

The boys gave me a terrible time, ragging me unmercifully and the whole thing became a bit of a joke. I even brought the clipping home to show Camille. But the first reaction on eagerly opening a paper and seeing a headline like that about yourself was devastating. The American Press, it seems have much more freedom of expression than ours!

Oh yes, and for all you Scots there was another laugh. Lynda finished by saying, 'Several weeks ago 137,000 spectators saw Moncur and his native Scotland team play the English national team in Hampden Park, Sussex.' So they've pinched our beloved ground now, have they?

Our baptism before a public which had about as much interest in soccer as I have in tiddlywinks was on Soldiers' Field. Now to anyone with a sporting knowledge that is a very famous place indeed. It was the venue for what most people consider the greatest and most controversial world heavyweight title fight in history.

On September 22, 1927 Gene Tunney beat Jack Dempsey there in the infamous battle of the long count. In the seventh round Tunney was down for at least fourteen seconds but got

Above: 'Off', says referee Joseph Minnoy as Inter Milan's goalkeeper is given his marching orders in last season's dramatic Fairs Cup-tie at Gallowgate. Seconds earlier the referee had been floored by a punch from the Italian. *Left:* One of my favourite photographs. Young Paul wears one of my international caps as Camille looks on

Helping our beauty queen Miss Magpie to hold the Fairs Cup is my mate John Gibson, who has helped me so much in producing this book

Two Welsh giants Mike England and Wyn Davies fight it out in the air

up again to win. 104,948 fans paid 2,658,660 dollars (at that time worth well over half a million pounds) for the privilege of witnessing the fight. With TV, radio and film rights it still stands as a record take for any sporting event.

Only about 5,000 spectators bothered to turn up to watch the new, peculiar sport of soccer on the day we were there but they saw an even bigger fight than the Tunney-Dempsey scrap. Saw it and took part in it! As we entered the stadium for our match with the Chicago All-Stars the Latin-American All-Stars were playing the Croation All-Stars, a bunch of Yugoslavs. It looked more like Custer's last stand than a football match with everyone hacking, kicking and punching each other. Suddenly over came a fan to run on to the pitch and banjo a player with as sweet a left hook as you like. The player, after looking amazed for a split second, set off in hot pursuit of his assailant clambering up the stand after him breathing fire and fury.

The game was forgotten. About half a dozen more fans raced on to the pitch to join in the full-scale battle waged by the players and the referee, wide-eyed and mouth open, waved his arms in despair abandoning the match. All of us were more than a little apprehensive knowing that we had to go on twenty minutes later and we decided that the best way to calm the situation was to give the crowd plenty of goals – as quickly as possible.

Within fifteen seconds Ron Guthrie had plonked the ball firmly in the Chicago net and before the final whistle went Bryan Robson and Keith Dyson had added two more each to give us a 5–0 victory. The fans loved it: they were happy again.

What with the fear of another riot and the wish to impress in our first game we showed probably our best form against local sides in that match. Later with the opposition a lot slower and less skilful we got a little casual and slap happy although always able to turn it on enough to win.

Soldiers' Field is one of the most peculiar pitches I've ever played on. Normally it is used for American football (nothing like soccer, of course) and is narrow and long. Consequently we seemed hemmed in by the touchlines but when the ball ran behind the goals it seemed to go on for miles.

It was the same in our only other game in America at Seattle much later in the tour only this time things were made even more difficult by the playing surface. We played on Astro turf which is a manufactured, all-weather surface used a lot in the States. Seattle was my first and last try on it and I've only one word to describe it: diabolical. Imagine playing football on coconut matting and you've got Astro turf. The ball doesn't skid as it does on ordinary turf it sticks and slows down. Consequently for the first ten minutes we did nothing but fall over the ball and the boss, sitting bare to the waist in scorching weather on the touchline, laughed until tears ran down his cheeks. Me? I felt like a boiled lobster and a circus clown all at once.

Every time you went down the artificial turf scorched and scratched your legs and to make matters worse Seattle were desperate to beat us. They stripped twenty-two players and kept bringing on substitutes every ten minutes. It was just like an ice hockey match with players running on and off. Each new player, of course, was fresh and bright and ran like the wind.

We managed to win 2–1 but it wasn't easy under the conditions. Their goalkeeper had a stormer although he saved some shots which would normally have flashed past him because they were slowed down by the turf. He wore glasses, too, which brought some dry comments about not being able to beat 'a bloody blind man'. Their goal brought the house down. We were a little slack at the back through not concentrating and this guy stuck home a good header. Up he jumped in the air to run round like Jair did when he scored against England in the World Cup. Everyone went wild and smothered him with congratulations. Poor old Iam was left scratching his head.

Our main base during the tour was in Vancouver. We stayed at the Georgian Towers Hotel where four of us shared a suite consisting of two double bedrooms, lounge, kitchen and the biggest fridge you've ever seen. I was with David Craig, Iam

McFaul and John Cowan and we worked it so that Craigy and Seamus were the cooks and Iam and me did the cleaning up. Mind you, Fanny Cradock needn't worry. The food wasn't great. More often than not we made do with a huge hamburger each which didn't exactly tax the imagination of the cooks!

We played the hosts Vancouver Spartans twice and the Victoria Royals twice: once in Victoria on the only real soccer pitch we saw and once on Nanaimo Island. Spartans, bossed by a guy called Bob Christopher, were the best local team we met by far. They operate in the Western Canadian League and in our first meeting almost caused an upset thanks to our party-spirit.

We accelerated to a two-goal lead in the first quarter of an hour thanks to Robson and Dyson and then relaxed to have some fun . . . only the Spartans didn't see it that way. In a quarter of an hour spell around half-time they cracked home three goals against a defence as wide as the Tyne to lead 3–2. Their coach Peter Dinsdale, the old Huddersfield player, was driving them on but we were secretly proud of our 100 per cent record and came back with goals from Robson and Young to pinch the match at 4–3.

During our stay in Vancouver I teamed up with a young lad called Kenny Mikkelson, who was Spartans' physiotherapist and also physio to the British Columbia Lions, an American football team. Kenny, only 19, helped out Dave Smith in our dressing-room and I've never seen anyone tape up ankles so quickly. He must be a wow at Christmas with all the parcels!

Training was pretty light-hearted stuff on the tour which was, to a certain extent, a working holiday after a strenuous season. As long as we won our matches the boss was happy. But this particular morning Dave Smith gave us hell for some reason. We trained on a ground overlooking the Pacific and he ran about like Emil Zatopek pushing us on and on until we were ready to drop. The lads were all pretty sick so I yelled across: 'Hey, Smithy once more round and we'll drop you in the drink.' Dave grinned and replied: 'You'll have to catch me first,' as he sprinted ahead of us.

I glanced over to Ollie Burton who got the message. Without warning we nipped across and whisked Smithy off his feet. He was laughing as we ran towards the water, confident that we wouldn't drop him in. But when I asked if he wanted to take his watch off he realised we meant it and began struggling.

'I can't swim, lads,' he yelled.

'Well, now's the time to learn,' I said dumping him in, track-suit and all. He thrashed about like a big octopus while the boss and us had a great laugh. In fairness Dave took it all in good part.

Our first match with the Royals was on Nanaimo Island and we did the journey in style. Four big Yankee estate cars were hired with the words 'beautiful British Columbia' blazoned across the number plates and off we went. It took us two-and-a-half hours on the ferry to reach the island and the capital Nanaimo. As with all the games we had to go through more pomp and circumstance than a Wembley cup final before we were allowed to get on with the ninety minutes' work.

Both teams marched out side by side and then lined up in front of the stand in one long crocodile line while an official appeared in front of us with a mike to make a spiel. Each player was introduced separately and we had to take one step forward and bow to the crowd. Boy, were we embarrassed. This day the speeches were longer than usual from the officials and one loud voiced drawled out from the middle of the stand: 'Get on with the game, man. We want action.' Trying to keep a serious face was difficult and our chairman Lord Westwood, who was next on the mike, came to the rescue by saying: 'Let's do what the man says. We all came to watch a game.'

Like most of the sides the Royals included a smattering of players with League experience back home. Player-coach was Brian Hughes, the former Swansea and Welsh international and Jim Menzies (Cowdenbeath), Peter Wilson (Wolves) and a Scottish schoolboy international Bill Hamilton were also in the side. We won the first game in Nanaimo easily enough 3–0 but the return in Victoria was a little harder although we got home 2–1.

Six games and six wins brought the end of the tour for me although the boys still had to play one more game against Eintracht Frankfurt in Toronto. There had been some confusion over the dates of the tour before we set off and as a result Ollie Burton and I had already booked our holidays by the time things were completed. The club readily agreed to us flying home before the last game and so we accompanied the boys to Toronto and then began what became an almost never-ending journey back to Tyneside lasting twenty-two hours.

In many ways I was sorry to miss the last leg of the tour. I hadn't seen Toronto or Niagara Falls where the lads were due to have lunch in a huge mushroom-shaped restaurant overlooking the famous drop and the Eintracht match was a bit of a challenge as the Germans had already beaten Manchester United and Celtic in America. John Cowan and David Young were brought in at centre-half and sweeper for the game and to everyone's delight we won 4–0. The boss tells me that Jinky Smith was absolutely outstanding. His skills reached an almost unbelievable peak.

Looking back the obvious question is whether or not soccer will catch on in America and Canada. And to be quite frank I don't think it will. At least not to the extent it has here. I believe that basically Americans and Canadians are lazy people who like lazy sports. Baseball and American football are the two great games out there and both are what I would term lazy sports. Baseball is slower than cricket and American football is just as bad being riddled with formations and stoppages. How on earth can you call American football players athletes when they all weigh around 17½ stone? As far as I can see the only credentials necessary are to be big and strong and able to run fairly fast in short bursts which don't come very often. These big guys would die playing ninety minutes of soccer.

Americans love everything to be bigger and larger than life even in their sports. Teams must win 28–22 or something like that and the thoughts of a team winning 1–0 after an hour-and-a-half creases them. One American, saying why he didn't like soccer, told me: 'There is not enough scoring, man. Why don't you award four points for a goal, three for hitting the cross-bar, two for the post and so on? Make it exciting and big, man. That's the idea.'

Next we'll be having a mathematician sitting in the dug-out to work out the score!

15 The Fans

This is the time of the Bovver boy. And he's getting the soccer fan a bad name. Pick up your paper virtually any day of the week and you'll read of violence on the terraces or in a city after a match. It seems to be spreading like a disease.

Yet I feel we should keep a sense of proportion. Sure, there is trouble and nobody likes it. The sooner it is stamped out the better and the police are doing a grand job in keeping control. But let us remember one thing. The troublemakers are in the minority. They are a bunch of wild kids who use football as an excuse for gang punch-ups. They're not the real fans and I don't like to see the thousands of genuine supporters having their name smeared by the idiots.

Take our fans in Newcastle. To me they are the greatest. Their loyalty and their sacrifice both in time and money is fantastic. Whenever we play our people are there in masses – and that includes abroad. Often they make more noise than the home crowd. Their behaviour in the main is first-class. That is something of which the players and officials are very proud. In 1969–70 they were voted the best behaved supporters in the First Division over the whole season by a panel headed by Football League secretary Alan Hardaker. Responsible officials including referees give regular marks which are collated over the year. It is a serious award handled with thoroughness.

The season before against Glasgow Rangers in the semi-final of the Fairs' Cup our supporters, including the boistrous Leazes end, showed admirable restraint in the face of a riot started by Rangers' hooligans behind the Gallowgate goal. There were about 50,000 Geordies in the ground but they simply chanted: 'We want football' while police grappled with the Rangers lot in the middle of the park. The good behaviour of the Geordie certainly prevented a bad situation from getting worse. There are exceptions, of course. It's the same everywhere but I think we at Newcastle are lucky to have a huge following of sensible and serious-minded people – connoisseurs of football if you like.

As judges of the game only Liverpool's supporters in my opinion compare with ours. As at Anfield there is always applause or at least a generous buzz of appreciation for any good work by the visitors. And the players soon know it. Some clubs have to manufacture fans by using gimmicks. I don't think Newcastle United have ever had to do this. Even when the team was having a bad time gates compared favourably with most clubs. Our supporters have always died for success but their affection for the club has always drawn them in. It is their very nature to come. Their fathers came. And their fathers before them. Football is the main topic for miles around. It is a football place.

When things are not going well a supporter will stop you in the street and instead of shouting abuse he will say: 'What went wrong, Bob?' He is interested. You get the feeling that the supporters are fond, that Newcastle United is their life. Give them success and their adulation knows no bounds.

Europe has meant the world to them as it has to us. They thrive on the big occasion: they give us a goal start with their 100 per cent backing. And when we responded by bringing home the European Fairs' Cup at the first attempt they were superb. I will never forget that homecoming. Never as long as I live regardless of what big moments there may be still to come. This was my first and most intimate.

We had won the trophy behind the Iron Curtain in Hungary and as we were due to touch down at Newcastle Airport during the afternoon while everyone was still at work I think we all worried inwardly that it would be a big flop. A damp squib. No one said a word but it was there eating away at us inside.

We needn't have worried. As the plane taxied in we could

see them out of the windows. Black and white scarves and banners seemed to be everywhere: on top of the air terminal building, all round it, on the tarmac, everywhere. We had to fight our way through the building and out to the coach. A hundred hands reached forward to touch the cup I was carrying. It was pulled backwards and forwards. Almost wrenched out of my hand. But it was their cup. They had a right to feel it. People lined every inch of the route from the airport to the ground. Office girls hung out of third-floor windows, schoolchildren chased us on their bikes despite a police escort and old ladies with shopping bags waved their hankies in a salute.

At the ground it was chaos. The steps and surrounds were crammed and inside was almost as bad. Everyone was jostling for a look at the silver pot. It was a bit of a rough and tumble but the mood was friendly and happy. Those few moments in the directors' box were perhaps the most emotional. One or two speeches drowned by the roar of the crowd and then suddenly there I was conducting the fans as they sang happily of victory and success. They had waited fourteen years since the good old days for something like this to celebrate and they intended to make the most of it.

We showed the cup round the pubs and clubs a lot that summer. Half of Tyneside had a drink out of it and the other half had their photograph taken with it. And every moment was a joy. We had given the best fans in the world something they wanted and that felt good.

Our old supporters, of course, still compare us with their old favourites. They would like us to be like Hughie Gallacher but they don't mind us the way we are. Comparison with today's players is hypothetical but it is a good thing for football. As long as people talk the game will thrive. It is up to us to create our own traditions. And I think we will. Perhaps the future generations will be regaled with stories of Wyn Davies, Bryan Robson and even Bob Moncur.

16 Another Good Sport

Virtually every footballer I know has a second sport – that is another game where he can relax more and play merely for the hell of it without worrying too much about the result. Frank Clark is a good league cricketer, David Ford likes squash, David Craig and Ian Mitchell go for tennis, and so on.

My second love is the footballer's favourite, golf. I also enjoy bowls which is a bit different but golf is the game that fascinates me and takes the bulk of my leisure time. I'm a member of Tyneside Golf Club and play off a five handicap which isn't bad. It could be better if I really worked at it but I cannot afford to give it that much attention. It's only a hobby although it's easy to forget that.

Golf is one of the few games where you play against yourself and that is the sort of challenge I cannot resist. The game breeds fanatics and theorists. Look at the book shops and they are full of magazines telling you how to improve your swing, straighten your drive or sink your putt. And thousands of golf enthusiasts including myself flock to buy the word of revered men like Arnold Palmer, Jack Nicklaus and Gary Player. Deep down we all believe that one day we might be as good as Palmer, Nicklaus or Player. That's what we aim at. I'm as bad as the rest in a way. Football will always be the most important thing in my life. After all, it's my bread and butter. But I love winning golf tournaments as well. Two of my biggest kicks were winning the Professional Footballers' golf championship at Finchley in 1967 and a big *pro-am* tournament with Dave Thomas at Sundridge Park last October.

The Finchley win was something of a surprise even to me. I had teed off early and returned an 83 over the par 72 course.

It wasn't a bad effort but I didn't think much more about it as I changed in the clubhouse and went for a beer. I expected it to be beaten.

As other players came in and told their scores I began to preen myself a little. Team-mates Bryan Robson and Gordon Marshall had an 86 and 88 respectively, Henry Newton of Nottingham Forest had 89 and so on. My return was beginning to look good – but still not a winner. At least in my eyes.

A couple of more beers slipped down before Barry Mealand, Fulham's full-back, strolled in.

'What have you done, Barry?' someone yelled.

'Eighty-three,' he replied. 'I picked up a couple of penalty strokes for lost balls on the 13th and 14th.'

Even then it didn't dawn on me that we had tied for the lead until an official elbowed his way through to the bar and started jabbering about a play-off.

There I was sitting in my ordinary togs enjoying a nice cold beer in the comfort of the clubhouse and they wanted me to go out and play again.

'I don't know about you but I'm not changing back,' I said looking at Barry.

'Fair enough,' he grinned.

So out we went in our everyday wear. Cuff links, suits . . . the lot. The only concession we made was to wear our golf shoes. It was sudden death . . . and I pinched it. My par four on the 310-yard first beat Mealand's five to give me the title I never expected.

But I still didn't pick up the first prize of £25. Instead I got a mere fiver. Before the play-off Barry and I agreed we would split the £40 prize money for first and second place down the middle whoever won. And my twenty quid was further divided by four because on the car journey down to Finchley Marsh, Robo, Bobby Cummings and I had decided to pool any winnings. We all had a chance and thought that we would share the cake. It was hard explaining to the missus on the phone that I was bringing home only a fiver instead of £25! Still, I got a handsome trophy for a year and a statuette for all time.

It still stands alongside my Fairs' Cup medal and other awards.

Mine was a second successive win for United – Bryan Robson had lifted the title twelve months before – but we were denied the chance of making it a hat-trick. The following year we were preparing for our first-ever game in Europe and I was recovering from a cartilage operation so no one was able to enter. I was a bit disappointed at not defending the trophy. Now there is no such competition which is a pity.

My *pro-am* win with Dave Thomas was a thrill because of the quality of the field. It's always nice to play with the big boys. I got my invitation through playing in another tournament a few weeks before. Bryan Robson and I were in the amateur section of the Whitley Bay Classic which fell just after the British Open and included such stars as Lee Trevino, the American who clowns his way round the course in Bob Hope fashion. George Will, the pro at Sundridge Park, was also there and he approached me to turn out in a big tournament at his club in aid of the Kent County Cricket Club Centenary Appeal Fund. The idea was that I would motor to Bromley after our home game with Arsenal on the Saturday, stay overnight with George, and play on the Sunday before motoring back.

I was pretty chuffed at being asked when I heard who else was due to play. The golfers were Neil Coles, Brian Huggett, Tommy Horton, Thomas and Will while Bobby Charlton, Mike England and Pat Jennings kept me company. Cricket was represented by such as Sir Len Hutton and Ken Barrington and showbiz personalities included Harry Secombe, Reg Varney and John Alderton. All the amateurs were fair golfers otherwise they would not have been chosen. The tournament was to be taken very seriously.

For the layman let me explain how things worked. Each pro went round with a footballer, cricketer and showbiz personality. He partnered each one with the lowest score at each hole going down on the card. Our quartet consisted of Dave Thomas, Sir Len Hutton, comedian Reg Varney and myself. Dave, who was born on Tyneside incidentally, really set us all up by scorching round in 64 to equal the course record. He burned off the opposition and it was merely a matter of which one of his partners produced the best supporting role. I bettered Dave's score at five holes which meant we had a net 59 which won the day. I hadn't played bad golf for an amateur and for us to finish three shots ahead of the rest of the field gave me a lot of satisfaction.

Reg Varney is a real nice fella. He has no edge about him or any of the falseness some people in show business seem to cultivate. He chatted his way pleasantly round the course and when he drove particularly well off one tee to win an approving comment the star of TV's 'On the Buses' grinned cheekily and said: 'You should have expected that – I'm a driver, aren't I?'

Most of the lighter moments came from Reg and John Alderton, of 'Please Sir.' John got the crowd of about six or seven thousand in a good mood right from the start. On the first tee after George Will had driven off they crowded round tight on the three sides. The guy on the microphone asked the crowd on the right to move back a little reminding them that John wasn't a professional. A guffaw of laughter came from the section behind John, who immediately wheeled round brandishing his club and snarled: 'You lot aren't safe either!'

Playing to the gallery is something that always goes down well in golf and this time was no exception. Mind you, I've known moments when people literally haven't been safe when the boys have been playing. Two instances in particular stand out in my mind. One happened at Carnoustie, the best course I've played on in Britain and I've played a few. We were approaching the famous seventeenth hole that borders one of the holes on the Burnside course. Alan Thompson, faced with the obstacle of two burns to clear, drove strongly off the tee but while his shot had power it lacked direction being slightly to the left.

In the distance a good 250 yards away the greenkeeper was sitting on his tractor totally oblivious to everything going on around him as he cut the fareway on the Burnside course.

Suddenly Alan's golf ball struck the tractor such a blow on the side. The driver almost died. His eyes bulged like Marty Feldman's as his head swivelled round and round to see where on earth the ball had come from. The hilarious part was that the ball ricocheted off the tractor back onto our fareway which meant Alan had played a shot which covered two courses! While we were falling about with laughter Alan said haughtily: 'I don't see what's funny – I played for that deliberately, you know.'

David Craig was 'danger man' in our next near-fatal accident, this time at Seaton Carew. The boys had organised a knock-out competition (appropriately as it turned out) and Bryan Robson was standing on one tee addressing the ball while Craigy was approaching the previous green. David's shot caught Pop in the most painful part of the anatomy on the bounce and Pop went down like a log. Craigy turned white and dropped his club to sprint across to where Pop was lying on the tee in a crumpled heap. I've never seen David move so fast in his life. What a knock-out tournament that was!

Actually, we've got some good golfers at our club. Pop was off three, before his transfer to West Ham earlier this year, I'm off five, the boss off seven and Craigy off eight or nine. Wyn Davies and Willie McFaul are also pretty handy and young John Craggs is becoming a fanatic. It is often said that golf doesn't help a footballer. The terrific amount of walking is supposed to slow you down and sap your strength. But I believe this only applies to youngsters who are liable to out-grow their strength anyway. The boss stopped me playing on certain days when I was a teenager and of course he was right but later on I played in a tournament with my club, Tyneside, every Thursday night with his permission.

I'm sure I could play on a Friday as well without it affecting my game on a Saturday providing I did it regularly. This is the secret, I think. If your muscles are used to it a round of golf will not affect you. It's only the occasional round that does the damage. And I like to play far too often for anything to happen to me.

17 Gallowgate's Characters

Gallowgate has had its fair share of big names in my time... men who simply couldn't be ignored. For one reason or another they were colourful characters who stirred the imagination of the public.

Think of men like Jimmy Scoular, Charlie Mitten, George Eastham, Alf McMichael, Stan Anderson, Jim Iley, Ron McGarry, Jimmy Greenhalgh, Alan Suddick and John McGrath and you will know what I mean. Today we still have 'em in the shape of Wyn Davies, Jim Smith and John McNamee.

But to the fans one man stands out as king of the clowns... a joker supreme. I refer to Ron McGarry, who regaled us all with his ready wit from 1962 until 1967. Even today there's no getting away from the McGarry humour for he's back training with us while playing for Barrow in the Fourth Division. In between times he's been Down Under making the Aussies stand on their heads. As player-coach with Balgownie he cracked home 35 goals from right-half in a season. 'I was so good they thought I was the new Messiah,' he quipped on his return. 'It got that bad I had to come back: the rest of the players were forming a lynching party because I was spoiling things for them!'

Like all comedians McGarry has a catch phrase. His is 'I'm the Greatest,' and he reckons Cassius Clay pinched it from him. To the unenlightened his humour probably does sound big-headed. In fact he's anything but. He's the most likeable, easy-going, generous sort of bloke who in reality is poking fun at himself. To Ron life is one big belly laugh and he likes others to laugh with him. Ask him to sum up his success in football and he'll say: 'I owe it all to being a good club man

– the Dolce Vita, the Cavendish and Greys!' All are nightclubs where McGarry is probably a better turn than the comedian on stage and where on the occasions he visits them he is better than a PRO. It was the boss, Joe Harvey, who discovered Ron and gave him to the soccer world as a kind of Bob Hope, Eric Morecambe and Ted Ray rolled into one. The boss was in charge of Workington then and McGarry was in the Army. Ron was quick to give up square bashing for football . . . and just as quick to give up football for Rugby League when he found that the expenses were better!

'He scored goals for us right from the start,' says the boss, 'but one day he went missing and I wondered where the hell he was. Then I found out on the Monday he had played Rugby League because they were more generous in meeting his expenses. That was it – I had to sign him pro on the spot before he became another Billy Boston.'

McGarry has always been the tough type of centre-forward who could take a lot of stick and dish it out as well. In our promotion season he did a magnificent job for us finishing as top scorer with 16 goals. I remember on one occasion he was having a particularly tough time with a centre-half who looked more like Desperate Dan than a footballer. However Ron was still getting past him pretty regularly and as half-time was coming up Mr Tough Guy was getting really sick. As McGarry steamed down the middle once again, the centre-half lunged into the tackle bringing Ron down with a tremendous thud and burying his face in the squelchy mud. 'That'll teach you, you b——,' he snarled. 'You can't run without legs.' 'Oh, yeah?' came the reply from McGarry spitting out mud. 'That's what you think, big mouth. I've got another set of bloody legs in the dressing-room to screw on at half-time!'

A giggle always helps to ease the tension and Ron often provided it. At Coventry Newcastle were losing 4–0 at half-time one day and the lads trooped in feeling utterly dejected. Stan Anderson flopped down next to McGarry looking particularly fed up when suddenly he felt an arm round his shoulder.

I'm only 8 but I'm already keen enough. That's me third from the left in the front row of my lifeboys' team

Left: Here I am proudly holding the Champions' Cup I won at Kirkliston back in 1955 when I was 9 years old. *Bottom:* You can almost feel the power as our right-half Tommy Gibb shoots for goal

Above: I look more like a heavyweight boxer than a professional footballer here and Paul doesn't seem too sure either. The photograph was taken after Camille met me at the airport after a particularly hard Fairs Cup match. *Below:* Newcastle *v* Liverpool: always a good match. Keith Dyson climbs above Chris Lawler to head for goal

'Cheer up, Stan,' grinned Ron. 'We're bound to get a draw. We've got the wind behind us this half.'

Jimmy Greenhalgh, our coach in the McGarry era, was Ron's one big rival in the laugh stakes. A similar dressing-room quip to the Coventry one also dispelled a lot of tension at the right time. This time it happened at Nottingham when Greenhalgh, a great thinker about the game as well as a ready wit, gave us a long tactical talk. Everyone was feeling a bit tense and anxious but Jimmy killed all that when, at the end of his spiel, he said: 'and remember, lads, for goodness sake don't let them panic you into playing football.'

He was a laugh a minute, Jimmy, but also a damned good coach. In fact I haven't come across a better one. He did a tremendous lot for the players who worked under him and that includes me.

Today we don't have quite the same jokers in the pack but we have the characters. Take John McNamee for example. The big fella who plays alongside me wouldn't look out of place with Lee Marvin in a western. Built like a combine harvester, when he scowls he can scare the living daylights out of you. And Mac revels in his image of a tough guy on the field. Off it he's more of a gentle giant with a quiet but infectious sense of humour. Mac has a story about virtually every centre-forward he's faced in the First Division and often passes the time away on train journeys by reciting a few of 'em. One of the best concerns his Boxing Day set-to with Allan Clarke, Leeds United's costly leader. After a particularly bruising battle Mac caught Clarke in the small of the back near full time. In the bath afterwards one of the lads referred to the incident and said it looked like a pretty tough clash. 'Aye,' said Mac with a slight grin. 'I've asked him to post my studs on to me when he's had them pulled out of his back.' Actually the clash hadn't been as bad as it looked. While Mac is extremely tough in the tackle he isn't deliberately dirty like some players.

Another of his famous 'taming' stories is about big Derek Dougan, as rare a character himself as you will find anywhere. Mac and the Doog spent all afternoon at the park grappling with each other like two mountain cats and at the end of it all John turned round to one of the boys and said with a twinkle in his eye: 'I'm off across the road now to wrestle Masambula!' New St James's Hall was opposite the football ground in those days and used to put on regular Saturday night wrestling bills starring Masambula, the African witch doctor.

Characters in a much different sense of the word are Jim Smith and Wyn Davies, the two costliest player's in Newcastle's history. Neither are jokers like the others I've talked about but they both rivet the attention of the public with the sort of magic that is indefinable and isn't solely to do with football talent.

Smith, or 'Jinky' as we call him because of his style, doesn't realise how good he is. With his skills he should be a world-beater: a regular in the Scotland international side. But Jinky is a soccer tantaliser in more ways than one. He can torment the fans, the management and his own team-mates just as easily as he can torment an opponent simply because he allows his form to be so erratic. As a bloke he is pleasant and easy-going without allowing you to get deep inside him. His trade-mark is that slow smile of his that creeps across his face when something amuses him. Like the day I received a letter from Scotland. It was shortly after I made the international team regularly and the writer said that previously Aberdeen and Jim Smith had been her favourites but now I was also a favourite. I tossed the letter over to Jinky who was getting changed for training. He glanced at it casually then said with a smile: 'I suppose you'll be framing it and showing it to your mother.' That remark had a touch of the real McGarry about it.

Jinky shares the same digs as Wyn Davies in Pelton, county Durham which makes for some household. Not much short of £200,000 worth of soccer talent under one roof isn't bad. Davies in many ways is different to Jinky although he still has something of the loner in him. Underneath he is a shrewd man who makes the most of his position as a top star (and something of a controversial one) to make sure he won't be in financial difficulties when his playing career is over. Wyn himself has a laugh at the remark of his Welsh international teammate Terry Hennessey about his business deals. After one particular stroke of money-making, Hennessey said: 'I think Wyn intends to buy bloody Caernarvon Castle to live in when he retires!' Caernarvon is Wyn's home town, of course.

One story that got round last season about Wyn and I was really upsetting. It was suggested that the Newcastle camp was split into two cliques: the Moncur clique and the Davies clique. And it implied that we didn't get on. Such a suggestion is ridiculous and damaging. Sure, we've had our rows. This game makes for a difference of opinion. But we've never held anything against each other. In fact I would say I get on better with Wyn now than I ever have since he arrived on Tyneside in 1966. We may have different interests outside football – for example Wyn likes horse racing and I don't – but just because we prefer to follow our own paths doesn't mean we don't speak. No one ever said eleven footballers must go round together socially like a herd of sheep.

As a player Davies receives almost as much criticism as praise. But here again I must defend him. He is a very important commodity to Newcastle United. It is not only a matter of what he can do with that head of his but what influence he has on the other team. Often he destroys them almost before a ball is kicked.

Forking out thousands of pounds on players like Smith and Davies is a serious business but even the transfer side of the game can have its amusing moments at Gallowgate. Take the time big John McGrath was transferred to Southampton. Their manager Ted Bates was in the boss's office trying to clinch the deal. As the boss lounged back casually in his chair Ted paced the floor, a worried look on his face. Finally the boss couldn't stand it any longer, 'For God's sake, Ted, sit down or I'll put another five hundred quid on the fee for a new carpet,' he snapped.

Those are the moments that make soccer the great game it is.

18 The Future

Now we come to the last chapter and an inevitable look into the future. What happens when I stop playing? Although that appears to be a long way off at the moment I have thought about it a lot. And I have come to the conclusion that I want to stop in the game – but only as a manager. I don't want to be a coach or chief scout, full time or otherwise. I want to be the boss making the decisions and living or dying by them. Rather than not have that I would get out of the game I love and lead a normal, ordinary life.

United's three regular skippers before me all made the transition exactly the way I would like to. Stan Anderson, Jim Iley and Jimmy Scoular all became player-managers with smaller clubs. They used their name and playing ability as a stepping stone if you like. That is the way for me, not two or three years as a coach with the chance of being forgotten at the end of it instead of being promoted. I want to cash in straight away. Jump in at the deep end. If I swim fine. If I don't there are a few million guys around making a living outside of soccer and I'm sure I could do the same.

There are pitfalls in soccer management, of course. It is a lonely life filled with responsibility but I've already told you how I feel about that. Being a skipper and playing in international football helps a lot in several ways. You learn about responsibility, about making decisions which are not always popular, and about man management. You learn how to speak in public, handle the Press and even deal with directors. It is a foundation, nothing more, but at least it gives you some idea of what management must be like.

The big difference between being a player and being a

manager is that a player holds his future in his own hands (or should it be feet?) while a manager's future is in the hands of eleven other people on a Saturday afternoon. But the way I see it those eleven players will almost certainly be men of your choice and if you choose carefully looking for character as well as football ability you must have a chance. The big axe always looms larger than life, of course. Newspapers are always telling us that Joe Bloggs is the 555th manager to be sacked since the war. You must be prepared to move round the country from job to job if necessary.

I've been lucky in my footballing life so far. Although I left home at the start of it I've never moved since. I've been on Tyneside around ten years or so now and have married a local girl and raised a family. Uprooting everyone would be something new and, I must admit, not particularly encouraging. But we would be prepared to do it.

Mind you, it's possible to hit lucky and not have to. Look at Stan Anderson: a legend in the North-east but not known all that well outside it. Stan spent all his playing career with Sunderland, Newcastle and Middlesbrough and is now Middlesbrough's boss. There isn't a missing link in the chain. I think the secret is that he kept his name respected in the area by playing with dignity and living the same way. And it has brought dividends.

If I could do the same thing I would be more than happy but I admit it's asking a lot to be lucky enough to stay in one area all the time. Football is the only thing I know. If I moved out I would be starting again from scratch.

Looking back I know it was a risk coming straight into soccer from school with no trade or profession to fall back on: no night schools and no GCE passes to bolster my chances of success in the world. I was football daft and I deliberately gambled everything on being a success in the game. It was a calculated risk and it came off. I shudder more now when I think about it than I did then probably because I'm older now and a family man. It's the old business of responsibility. Obviously I still have nothing concrete to fall back on outside the game. But I have a name. And I intend to keep it clean. A name and a reputation – that's something. If you have average intelligence – and I hope I have that – you should be able to get by with the right sort of help.

Football has been good to me. Very good. It has enabled me to buy my own house and get a car for my wife as well as myself. It's brought a good standard of living and an enjoyable social life. A bit of fame although not exactly a fortune. Having got so much out of it, I want to put some back and as a manager I could do that. But don't suggest I am going to become a second Joe Harvey. I've never consciously modelled myself on anyone although some of the boss must have rubbed off on me after so many years with him.

No, I want to be the first Bob Moncur. Nothing more. Nothing less. I'll take my own chance at a shot at the top.

See you in the stocks!

Index